CELEBRATION
IN THE BEDROOM

"*Then God created male and female,
and it was excellent in every way.*"

—from Genesis 1

CELEBRATION
IN THE BEDROOM

Charlie Shedd
Martha Shedd

WORD BOOKS
PUBLISHER
4800 WEST WACO DRIVE
WACO, TEXAS
76703

ISBN 0–8499–0171–5

Library of Congress Catalog Card Number 79-66409

Unless otherwise indicated, Scripture quotations are from
the King James Version of the Bible. Those marked TLB
are from The Living Bible, Paraphrased (Wheaton: Tyn-
dale House Publishers, 1971) and are used by permission.
Scriptures marked RSV are from the Revised Standard
Version of the Bible, copyright 1946, 1952, © 1971, 1973
by the Division of Christian Education of the National
Council of the Churches of Christ in the U.S.A., and used
by permission.

Printed in the United States of America

Contents

A Personal Word From Charlie & Martha

Have you ever noticed this interesting item from the first chapter of Genesis?

When God made the light, it was good.

The earth and seas were good.

So was the vegetation, good.

Ditto for the sun, moon, and stars.

The creatures of the sea and the birds were good.

The animals were also good.

Then after God created male and female, the words are, "Behold, it was *very* good."

The Living Bible says, "So God made him like his Maker. Like God did God make man; Man and maid did he make them. . . . Then God looked over everything he had made and behold it was *excellent* in every way" (Gen. 1:27, 31 TLB).

The Good News Bible: "He was very pleased."

Amplified Version: "And He approved it completely."

On a scale of one to ten, ten for perfect, how do you grade your sex life against the two words "very good"?

If you get eight or nine, hurry, go write a book. But if your rating is below five, tune in right here.

Celebration in the Bedroom is the word of a couple who believe that sex at its best is a matter of tuning in together to the Lord.

For thirty-nine years prayer has made all the difference in the marriage we know best. If we believe what the Bible says, then we as Christians should be society's most liberated people, the super celebrators of sex.

You will see that our book is organized around five of our favorite prayers, and it is our hope that you may be inspired to work out your own prayers. For us, this is a fact:

The more we pray,
the more we know
what the Bible means
when it says:
"Then God created male and female . . . and
he looked over all that he had made, and behold
it was excellent in every way."

Which of these words best describe your attitudes toward sex? (Check several)

wonderful ___		uninhibited ___	
questionable ___		hung up ___	
positive ___		aggressive ___	
negative ___		hesitant ___	
pure ___		restful ___	
repulsive ___		tiring ___	
obligation ___		exciting ___	
celebration ___		dull ___	
healthy ___		fascinating ___	
harmful ___		routine ___	

Holy ___

Having inventoried yourself, now check those words you feel most accurately describe your mate. If your marriage is ready for it, you might have an interesting session as you compare individual findings.

For an effective relationship, sooner or later there must be an understanding of these four things:

1. Where I am in my head and heart;
2. Where *you* think I am;
3. Where you actually are;
4. Where *I* think you are.

Always in marriage we do well to come into our dialogue laying aside the question: Is she right or am I? Is he wrong or am I? Instead we must launch our communication in the spirit:

Lord, help us to understand each other;
To appreciate each other's thoughts;
To feel each other's feelings.
Take over completely in our hearts and make
us sensitive with the sensitivity of Christ.

Amen

I

LORD, *help us think of sex*
as you first thought of it,
a gift to celebrate,
excellent in every way.

"Yes," "No," and "Whoopee"

A psychiatrist friend of ours makes this statement: One test of emotional health is the ability to say "Yes," "No," and "Whoopee."

Some people find it hard to say even a timid "Yes." Others who have trouble saying "No" lack the courage to take a firm stand. For some of us "Whoopee" may not have quite the right sound. In certain areas of our history this word has risky connotations.

But "Whoopee" at its best
    for those who know it at its best
        means very much the same as "Praise the Lord."
"Praise the Lord for being alive."
    "Praise the Lord for male and female."
        "Praise the Lord for all things good in
            every way."

"But I Don't Want to Be Sexy"

She came into our room looking very much like a woman bent on seeing the manager. She had been attending one of our seminars and was thoroughly turned off. Especially in the section on married sex she had slammed the inner doors, closed her mind to anything new, shut her heart to even the slightest change.

13

"But I don't want to be sexy," she announced, "and I don't want anybody to tell me I ought to be sexy. For sure, I don't want anyone *religious* telling me I ought to be sexy."

Then on and on she went in grim recital, "Of course, I love Dick. I promised him that when I married him. But you can't fool me. Most men are all out for everything they can get. They're animals, that's what they are. All the time thinking about sex, nothing but sex . . . et cetera, ad infinitum."

What could we do with Ruth? Nothing. What could Dick do with Ruth? Nothing. What could the Lord do with Ruth? Nothing.

Repeatedly the Bible makes this clear: God cannot do anything for those who will not let him. By his amazing courtesy he allows us to stand behind our barricade forever if that is our choice.

So what does this say about celebrating sex? What it says is that we must believe God wants us to celebrate sex. He wants us to open up, to be willing.

Prayer for the Cleanup Squad

For most of us sexual celebration at its finest will require some adjustments. Having accepted the truth that God made sex and made it good, we may need some background work in our hearts and in our heads. Rising above our early training could be an awesome challenge.

The vacuum of our parents' silence will need to be forgiven and whispered negatives forgotten. Old sins, unfortunate experiences, false concepts, grudges, memories making us nervous—all these must be faced, released, surrendered, and left with the Lord.

In some cases even the church's victorian positions will need to be reexamined. Where they have affected us adversely, these too will require research, understanding, and rejection. Earnestly, honestly, thoroughly, we must pray,

> "Lord, there are so many roots to our hangups. Send your cleanup squads and prepare our souls, our minds, our bodies for celebration of your love .... Amen."

"I Made Myself a Sexual Person"

Rachel: "My problem was I never thought about sex, and it seemed like my husband never thought about anything else. So I actually forced myself to think 'sex,' and it's amazing how many sexual images there are in the world if you look for them.

I made myself a sexual person. I believe you can do that. By concentrating you can guide yourself into thought processes which make you that way. I don't think I was turned off by sex, just sort of blah.

So if there are any of you who wonder, can I make myself sexy, I know you can. And if you were to ask my husband, he would say, 'You sure can, praise the Lord.' "

> *Virginia:* "I have told Arnie that I am ready to try anything sexually he wants to try. But when I tell him, I always add: Don't expect me to warm up to all these new ideas immediately. You be patient and I'll be open-minded. You be gentle, and I'll be willing."

Two great statements, we think, from two very special wives.

Any Limits in Married Sex?

Often in our mail comes letters like this:

"My husband is always pushing me to try things I've never even heard of. I wonder if he's a little bit weird."

"If only my wife would experiment a little. She thinks there's only one way for sex, and I think we're missing a lot, because she won't let herself go."

So what are the limits?

Answer: There are none. Anything any couple wants to do in marriage, if it is not physically, mentally, or psychologically damaging can be a part of the celebration.*

Thought for meditation:

If God saw everything he had made and behold it was excellent in every way, who are we to question his creation?

For the Christian, there is one other limit. This is anything forbidden in Scripture. But concerning some of our questions, the Bible is not explicit. Then what do we do? If we are sincere in our desire to please God, we refer to The Living Word. We have this beautiful promise straight from the Book itself—the Spirit will guide us and some of us have found that the unity of our feeling is the most accurate guidance of all.

One Hundred and Forty-Seven Positions

One day we went into a bookstore and in our browsing we came on a title, *One Hundred and Forty-seven Posi-*

---

* Since this book is a book for Christian marrieds, we proceed on the basis that everything we are saying applies here to married sex. As we will see, for the Christian, adultery, fornication, group sex, exchanging partners, or sex outside the marriage by any other name, is not one of our options (Section II).

tions for Intercourse. We have a Japanese friend who says the Japanese are the world's most sexually sophisticated people. "Ah," says he, "the title is a put-on. There are only sixty-five positions and most of these are but variations of a basic six."

We bought *One Hundred and Forty-seven Positions for Intercourse,* brought it home, pondered, and we believe the Japanese are right, especially about that basic six.

Before we could study the book at length, we lent it to someone who needed it more than we did. For us it had little to say. The uninhibited can work out their own variations. Since the Lord made it excellent in every way, the best way is *our* way.

Frequency Questions

Among the most often asked questions in seminars, workshops, and via the postman are those which mean:

How often should a couple have sexual intercourse to qualify for healthy sex?

Usually it is the man asking, or the wife of a complaining man. But there is really no definitive answer, because every person is different and every combination of two people is different. Since this is true, the "frequency" question must have different answers.

One survey says nine times monthly. Another reports, "The norm is three times weekly with an occasional miss." But how do the surveyors know, and what difference does it make?

It doesn't make one bit of difference if once each week is right for us, or once each day. Or twice on Sunday. Or three times.

Question: What are the indicators that we are not getting what we need sexually?

Word from an astute wife: "I can always tell when we aren't sexually active enough, because we start sniping at each other. It's a fact. Both our temperaments are better when we're sexually active."

Lock on the Bedroom Door

Letter from a Wisconsin husband:
"This may sound silly. But my wife and I are having a big disagreement. We have three children, ages nine, seven, and four. Well, what the argument is over is that I say we should have a lock on our bedroom door and my wife says no. She thinks parents should never shut their children out, ever.

We really do get along great most of the time and I want you to know I pride myself on knowing what I'm doing. But I sure don't need an audience and I tell her she'd do better too without the threat of interruption. So what's the matter with a lock?"

Nothing.
Sex at its best needs full protection for free expression. In addition we have seen some negative leftovers in children who accidentally came on their parents in intimate moments.

God made sex so that it is very right when it is right. And for us one way to keep it right is to keep it private.

Nudity ... Ashamed of Our Nakedness?

"They were ashamed."
It's a sad note in Genesis 1, and from that day to this

many of God's children have been nervous about naked-
ness.

Letter from a disappointed husband:
"My wife has a sensational body and that's one
reason I married her. But I can't tell you what a
let-down it's been to discover that she has a real
hangup about nudity. I thought when a couple got
married, they should enjoy being nude together. But
not my wife. I tell her somehow I feel like I am missing out on the most beautiful sight in the world, but
she says she's just that way. Why is a woman that
way and is there anything I can do about it?"

The answer to question one is probably far back down
the road she's come. And until she is willing to backtrack
that road she may go on being overly prudish forever.

He's right. For a man who loves his woman, there
should be no more beautiful sight than the beauty of the
Lord in her original creation. Let's hope she can work it
out and come one day to realize God created male and
female and behold it was excellent in every way, including nude.

Many men would agree mountains are beautiful and sunsets; oceans, rivers, brooks, lakes,
each have their particular glory. Ditto for the
night sky, the stars, full moon. For the day sky,
too, sunrise, white clouds, the bird in flight,
rainbow, and the majesty of a storm.

Yet still with all these many splendors, some
of us would say, "I am married to the most
beautiful sight in the world. Thank you, Lord."

"Why Does My Husband Have This Thing about Oral Sex?"

Questions, questions, thousands of questions, millions in the minds of Christian people all over the land.

In marriage seminars we have one period when anyone is allowed to write a question on anything. Unsigned. They come in a nervous hand, sometimes tiny writing and often the tightly folded ones are asking:

> "What about oral sex?" .... "Is the use of the mouth all right?" .... "What does the Bible say about oral sex?"

"Fellatio" and "cunnilingus" * may have been strictly hush-hush in a day when our parents attended workshops. But not today. Oral sex has suddenly gone public, and many women are asking,

"Why *does* my husband have this thing about oral sex?"

We once heard a paper on "Subconscious Causative Factors in the Male Urge for Oral Intercourse." Sounds like a psychiatrist's title, and it was. He said, "In my experience it is almost always the male who makes the first proposal for oral sex. Most women have seldom, if ever, given it a thought. To them, even if they are sexually responsive in other ways, oral sex may sound strange. Let us examine the reasons why the male might be more inclined to oral sex than the female."

Putting his words in our words for simplification, this is what came through:

1. Every man has a subliminal urge to return to the womb.
2. Every man has a subliminal urge for total inti-

---

* "Fellatio" is the use of the female mouth on the penis. "Cunnilingus" is the use of the male mouth on the vagina.

macy, a longing for totality. He also has an innate curiosity to inspect.

3. Every man considers his penis a prized possession. In oral sex he is offering his best.

4. Every male somewhere in the years from infancy to youth was rejected somewhere . . . something was denied him . . . he couldn't do everything he wanted to do . . . "No" . . . "Stop it" . . . "You can't."

Now comes a premise difficult perhaps for laymen's comprehension, but again quoting the doctor: "In everyone there is a tendency to do a complete reverse on our early negatives. Someone denied us? See, we are denying nothing."

No one knows all the answers to all our human urges, but for those who have been wondering, the doctor's trip into regions less familiar might be worth some serious discussion. And especially for husbands, here's another word of wisdom, this one from a wife who represents the feelings of most women:

"The first time he approached me in this way, I thought I would come unglued. I had never heard of anything like this. And I was also one of those little girls brought up in a family where nobody ever mentioned sex, let alone talking about the sex organs. But I did know I loved my husband, so I said a prayer and the message I got was that if it's important to him, I better not act too shocked.

So that's how we got into it, and now it has become a pleasurable part of our love-making for both of us."

"Unsanitary?"

Straight from another doctor: "Contrary to most people's understanding, the penis and vagina are not unsanitary. God made them clean and healthy. In most cases it is the mouth where the germs are. So whatever the reasons for not having oral sex, germ possibilities of the sex organs are not authentic."

And from a clinical psychologist:

"There is a professed taboo in our society about oral love and that's too bad, because there can also be a nice kind of mystique here. The lips and tongue are extremely dexterous, soft, warm, and lubricated in such a way that they are very stimulating, producing effects which cannot be produced in any other manner."

What does the Bible say about oral intercourse?

Certainly there are texts which can be quoted as a ban against almost anything and everything. But in our opinion, those who would ban oral sex by biblical quotations are reading something into the Scripture which isn't there. Let's hear it again: when the Bible is silent, we accept that silence as one more indicator that God leaves some things up to us.

In our tuning in to the living Word, this is the message:

"Anything you both want to do
Anything you both enjoy
Anything not physically, mentally, nor
    psychologically harmful
Anything not forbidden in my Book
    Is excellent in every way."

One of the most unusual letters ever to come in our mail is this from a most extraordinary couple.

"We have something we want to ask you, because we heard a Christian doctor speak last week and what he said has bothered us a little.

One of our ways of making love is to go for a ride in the evening on country roads where there is little or no traffic, and while we ride along, we pet each other even to the point of mutual climax.

During this time we talk about our love. Almost always the way we do it, it is very slow and easy, quiet and gentle.

Sometimes we even do it on trips when we leave the freeway for a while and drive along a country road. I can't tell you what this means to us. We recently bought a new Chevy Caprice and one of the first things we did was to go for a ride and make love our way.

But the thing which has worried us is that the doctor said you should never pet to climax without the actual act of intercourse. So why not? For us it's beautiful, and we would appreciate your opinion."

We think it's beautiful too. For you. We also wonder if you may have misinterpreted the doctor's statement. This is what he probably meant: Those couples who are into sexual substitutes *exclusively* are making a mistake, missing too much, likely to get hung up on their substitutes. If you told that doctor what you've told us, we think he too might say, "Beautiful!"

"Then God created male and female,
   and behold it was excellent in every way."

Anticipation is another of God's good gifts. "I can hardly wait, tonight we celebrate."

What will she be wearing? One of my favorites, or nothing? How will she want me? Aggressive? Slow and sensuous?

Where will he want me? Upstairs? Downstairs? Somewhere on the carpeting? Which of our many ways? Soft, easy, slow, gentle, violent?

For the wise, talking about sex ahead of time, gradually turning up the thermostats can be another great part of great sex.

The Bible says, "Where there is no vision, the people perish" (Prov. 29:18).

One modern translation has it: "Where there is no forward look, the people become discouraged."

Ditto for sex.

Pornography and the X-Rated

"Dear Dr. Shedd:

My husband insists I go with him to X-rated movies. And I mean even the XXX hard-core films. He says it's a good thing, because it's stimulating. Frankly, I don't think we need any stimulation. We are both very young, and goodness knows I'm sexually alive.

Well at first I was repelled. Some of those things almost made me sick. So now it's nothing but a bore, and I told him I'm not going anymore.

He also likes girlie magazines and books with language you wouldn't believe. What makes a man like this? And do you think I am wrong to finally say, 'No?' "

You are not wrong to finally say, "No." Many people

feel as you do. For them pornography is an insult to their moral standards. Many others join you in your feeling of boredom. Some of the porn dealers are crying these days, because their business is falling off. We recently traveled in the Scandinavian countries and read a statement in one of their major city newspapers. Two reporters had been assigned to find out why sex magazines, sex items, and sex theaters were economically depressed.

Their conclusion: "The problem seems to be that there are only so many things a man and a woman can do to each other, and when you are surfeited with the viewing of these, what's left?"

Any wife has the right to continue a firm "no," while she insists that her husband find both professional and spiritual help to sort out his problem and clean up his mind.

And now another slant on boredom. This quote is from a girl, who before she became a Christian, acted in sex films. Her report:

"I cannot remember one time when I truly enjoyed sex, and most of the girls I knew who were into this sort of thing would tell you the same: and isn't it sad we got paid for something which looked like fun, but wasn't? Yet maybe even sadder is the fact that so many men paid their money for something so phony?"

Sound that note again: Real sex, satisfying sex, sex at its best is the long-range response of a husband and wife celebrating the goodness of divine creation.

Music

Report from imaginative lovers:
"My husband is a music teacher. He directs the choir at our church, and I sing in it. I also play the flute in the symphony and we thought you might like to know something we did. Maybe there will be another couple somewhere who would find it helpful.

We agreed that certain music has sexual connotations for us. So we talked about this and decided to record some of our favorite things, things that excite us most. We each made suggestions and my husband put them on a cassette.

Very often in the evening when we are reading, we will turn on our music for background mood. Or when we go to bed, we play it, and you know what happens.

I suppose different kinds of music would have different effects on different people. But for us this has been great. Sharing our selections and putting them together was good for us ahead of time, because it helped us find out so much about each other. Then when it becomes an adjunct to our love-making, it is positively beautiful."

High notes, low notes, gay roundelay or somber fugue; pianissimo, fortissimo; andante; allegro; loud and soft—play on.

"Excellent in every way."

Sex and Laughter

Gretchen, in one of our seminars: "Sex is the most fun you can have without laughing."

Beatrice: "I don't agree with you, Gretchen. With us sometimes sex is for laughs too. We giggle, and kid each other and joke. Why shouldn't all these be part of our sexual celebration too?"

From the same seminar, another comment: "Well, I agree with Gretchen. For my wife and me sex is all serious. We think it is much too sacred for anything frivolous."

> Say it again:
> To each his own.
> "Excellent in every way."

"Shouldn't We Be Slowing Down?"

Over and over and over, like a metronome, certain questions repeat themselves. Among these are the various versions of "will our sex run out as we get older?"

> "My husband says you shouldn't expect to be active at our age. We're sixty-four. Well, I can tell you I am still interested even if he isn't, and I get frustrated sometimes. He says he's the normal one. Can you tell me whether I really am abnormal?"

> *Answer:* You're not abnormal. You sound like a very healthy woman and your attitude is much healthier than your husband's.

"From somewhere my wife got the idea that after the menopause women don't enjoy sex any more. She says she's willing to go on with it whenever I need it, but that turns me off. It isn't true, is it, that women are out of it sexually after they've gone through the change of life?"

Answer: No, it isn't true and it is not at all abnormal for both male and female to enjoy sex as they grow older. But here's a note of warning: All the doctors we know agree that when sexual interest wanes, the sooner this disinterest is faced and dealt with, the more likely it is to be corrected. Experts say, "The way to keep sexually active in the future is to keep sexually active now."

Celebrating the Empty Nest

"Our daughter is graduating from high school next year. She is working in one of the national parks this summer and then away to college. I can't tell you how depressed I get when I think about the last of our children leaving home. Whatever will I do?"

Here is one answer:

"Our son is attending trade school two hundred miles away and since he's our only child, you'd think we'd be feeling down. But we're not. The truth is my husband and I have never had so much fun in all our lives. Think of it, absolute freedom at home to do what we want to do when we want to do it and not worry.

But here is one thing that does worry us. Many of our friends seem to go through a depression period when their children are gone and they are finally alone together.

One morning at breakfast my husband said, 'Do you think we're enjoying all this too much? Are we funny?'

We would appreciate knowing what you think."

Answer: We think you two are where you should be mentally and physically—free at last to celebrate. And you will like this line from one of our psychiatrist friends. He says,

> "When the last child leaves home, a new emotion sets in. It is called ecstasy."

The Strange, Bizarre, Peculiar

Sometimes in consultation and via the mail strange things surface: sadism; transvestism; voyeurism; and other miscellany outside our experience.*

It is evident that even in the bedrooms of Christian homes there will be deviations from what most of us would call "the norm."

A minister's wife comes questioning. The only way her husband can be sexually aroused is for her to dress up like a slave mistress, rattle some chains, crack whips, and play the cruel mistress. She says, "It really is not offensive to me and since we both need sex, I play his game. Of course, I wouldn't hurt him and he knows it. But the more I pretend, the better he likes it." This is a spiritually responsive woman, and she asks, "When you talk about sexual celebration in Christian marriage, is this too far out? My husband says he will never go for help. But you can see I am bothered, or I wouldn't be asking you."

Another wife writes: "My husband likes to dress up in women's clothes and sit around the house in the evening. We have two children and we make sure they never see him this way. I honestly don't mind. It doesn't do

---

*Sadism: stimulation by real or simulated cruelty. Transvestism: dressing in clothes of the opposite sex. Voyeurism: Sexual excitation by viewing.

anything for me, but it isn't repulsive either. And it seems to satisfy something in him. Would you tell me how you feel about this?"

We're really not the ones to give advice here. The reason? These things are outside the realm of our experience. To us they may sound kinky, but maybe they aren't.

We believe that couples wondering like this should go for professional help. And if one will not go, the other should.

We return to our premise: Anything any couple wants to do which is not physically, mentally, or psychologically damaging, and not forbidden in Scripture, is authentic for Christian celebration. To determine physical danger should not be difficult. But sometimes mental or psychological damage is not so easy to recognize.

Rule: Those who worry about these things should seek counsel.

One more thought for pondering, this from a marriage counselor with years of experience: "Sometimes the unusual sex, when not overdone, could actually be a safety valve. Before becoming too judgmental we need to ask ourselves, 'If we get them looking askance at what they are doing now, would they be into something worse?'"

Pronouncement in Pants Suit

During one of our seminars the problem of transvestism was brought out in our question and answer period. Immediately, an attractive young wife rose to quote Deuteronomy 22:5.

"See," she said, "it says here that God hates men who

wear women's clothes and women who wear men's clothes. That's our answer, isn't it?"

Interesting item: The ardent defender of living by Scripture was wearing an obviously expensive pants suit!

When we base our performance on biblical admonition, we must allow plenty of room for variant interpretation. What did the writers mean in the original? Were they talking about undergarments only? Even in Jesus' day men wore robes, and what did the women wear?

Scripture As a Preparation for Sex

It was an exciting day for us when this message came through: sex is God's gift for our celebration. And the more we put our ear down to Scripture, the more these celebration notes came loud and clear. One example is the Song of Solomon.

Our professor of Hebrew at the seminary was fond of saying, "If the government knew what was in *The Song of Solomon,* they wouldn't let a Bible go through the mail." Which being interpreted means, "Here we have an ultrastimulating book."

Recommendation: Read this little gem of the ancient Hebrews en toto. Then read it again with an eye to sexual undertones and overtones. Now make a collection of those phrases you find most exciting. Read them aloud to each other. Ponder. Muse. Let yourself go in the word of the Lord.

Here are some of our favorites:

> Your rounded thighs are like jewels,
>   the work of a master hand. . . .
> Your two breasts are like two fawns,
>   twins of a gazelle.
> How fair and pleasant you are.

31

O loved one, delectable maiden!
You are stately as a palm tree,
  and your breasts are like its clusters.
I say I will climb the palm tree
  and lay hold of its branches.
Oh, may your breasts be like clusters of the vine . . .
  and your kisses like wine
  that goes down smoothly
  (Song of Solomon 7:1, 3, 6–9 RSV).

As the apple tree among the trees . . .
  so is my beloved among the sons.
I sat down under his shadow with great delight
  And his fruit was sweet to my taste. . . .
His left hand is under my head
  And his right hand doth embrace me. . . .
My beloved is mine, and I am his:
  he feedeth among the lilies
  (Song of Solomon 2:3, 6, 16).

Students of the Bible know that there are many other stimulating passages throughout both Old and New Testaments. Combining these may be exactly what is needed for ultra celebration.

II

LORD, we commit to you our thoughts,
our eyes, our urges,
and we pledge ourselves
to absolute fidelity.

Cleave As in "Cemented Together"

"Cleave" is a plain vanilla word straight from the lips of Jesus. Two of the gospel writers record his use of it in reference to marriage. In our study together we have decided that whenever the Scripture repeats itself, we should pay double attention. Twice we read:

"For this cause shall a man leave
father and mother, and shall cleave
to his wife"
(Matt. 19:5; Mark 10:7).

We are to "cleave." And any student of the Bible knows that many of Jesus' teachings take in both genders. Men are to cleave, and women too. "Adhere, cling, stick, hold fast, cemented"—these are but a few of the synonyms used in our dictionaries.

So this is our directive straight from Jesus:

"We are forever cemented together
in absolute fidelity. In countless
ways, including sexual, we belong
exclusively to each other."

Fantasies and the Roving Eye

Absolute sexual fidelity does not mean that we will be free of urges, fantasies, fleeting thoughts of extramarital encounters.

Young wife: "I kid you not, when it comes to female bodies, Johnny has a measuring tape in his head."

Martha: "Charlie, too, and at first that was hard for me. But when I made friends with it, I learned to like it. And after getting it in perspective, I told him, 'Maybe this isn't the best when it comes to biblical scholarship, but let's say it isn't a sin if you can tell me what you're thinking.'

So now we make a game of it, and for us it's one of the fun things we do.

We live on a beach where women swim in bikinis, stroll in bikinis, loll in bikinis, and if a woman can relax, it won't take long to learn what her man especially likes. It didn't take me long either to realize that most of the time what my man likes is almost everything about every kind of woman.

So we walk along, evaluate the various arrangements of molecules, laugh, talk, and love each other in this very special way.

But I am also free to tell him what I'm thinking, what I like, what looks good to me. That's fair, isn't it? In any game we think the rules apply both ways.

I know some women whose husbands aren't interested in anything sexual any more, and I always feel a special sadness for them.

Do you suppose being honest with each other, surfacing our fantasies, could be one of the reasons why sex goes on getting better and better?"

"Thank you, Lord, for a love so meaningful that all our little turn-ons can be turned into an even greater turn-on at home."

"O Brother, Do I Wonder!"

"Dear Dr. Shedd:
Do I have the dirtiest mind in the whole wide world? To be perfectly honest, some of the things I think scare me. Why am I like this? I'm happily married. I don't think I'd ever cheat on my wife. I call myself a Christian and I really want to be. I'm an officer in my church. I like to believe I'm a good man, morally. But O brother, do I wonder!"

So what shall we say?

Most men would say, "Join the club. I worry too." But it helps to know that others struggle like we do. Yet it helps even more to accept this struggle as a natural part of living. Most of us had a mighty battle with out fantasies prior to marriage. And most of us, when we're honest, would admit that the mere act of marriage did not wave some magic wand to speed fantasies away.

Fact: When the Lord gives us a vision of what life can be with each other, he doesn't blind us to other possibilities.

Let's flash back here to that casual comment: "I am also free to tell him what I'm thinking. That's fair, isn't it?"

It certainly is.

"Anthony and I are happily married and we have a good thing going every way, including sex. But sometimes I have fantasies about other men, especially about the boy I was engaged to in college. I'm glad I didn't marry him, but I still have these bothersome flashes. They are only temporary, but very real. Somehow I wish I could tell Anthony about this. Do you think

37

it would take something away from our relationship if I did?"

It shouldn't. Maybe Anthony has some hidden thoughts he'd like to share. Psychologists say the healthiest minds are those which can surface their thoughts to one other person. When that person can be the person we love, two positive things result:

A. We become healthier individuals;

B. Our relationship is strengthened.

The Bible says, "The Lord knoweth the thoughts of man . . ."; "He knoweth the secrets of the heart" (Pss. 94:11; 44:21).

That's a scary piece of news when we comprehend it fully. But it's also good to know that he knows our thoughts and loves us anyway.

And it is also good, so very good, to be able to pray: "Thank you, Lord, for someone on the human level who knows my humanness, understands, and goes on loving me."

Courage in the Doctor's Office

Frequent question: "But what can I do? I have these urges and I know God gave them to me. I also know the Ten Commandments and anybody knows what the word 'no' means. How can I say 'no?' "

Straight from our mail comes this amazing story of courage in a doctor's office.

"Dear Dr. Shedd:

Very often in my practice as a family physician a couple comes to me where one or the other has had an affair. Usually, it's the man, and when I see them sweating it out, I know most of them wish it had never happened.

Well, I know one way to prevent it, and that's why I decided to write you. I thought it might help someone else like it did me.

Last year I became interested in one of my assistants. I should tell you that I am married and have three children. My wife and I consider we have an above average marriage. But still there was this strong attraction and it was very mutual. My assistant also is married and she admitted she was having a problem too.

So what we did was to have a head session together where we drew up an agreement, and it goes like this:

1. If we can help it, we will never be alone together with the door closed. If it has to be closed, it will never be locked.

2. We will never touch each other. No physical contact.

3. We will tell our mates about our feelings and show them this agreement. (Fortunately for us, they are both mature people.)

4. If we can't live by these three rules, we will part company.

The bottom line is that we have been working together this way for over a year now, and we both know this simple agreement has kept us from any destructive over-involvement."

We think that is greatness. Cast a special medal for special courage.

It's More Fun to Be Good

When I was a boy Judge Evans lived up the road from our house. He was a wise old barrister who took a special interest in me. I think he sensed that I would be needing all the help he could give me.

So he would take me down in his basement study for what he called lessons one, two, six, seven, and into the hundreds. How he kept count I don't know, but I do know that whenever it was something ultra-important, he called it Lesson 777. There were any number of these, but one I remember especially well was:

"The Lord has put us together so you can count on this—keeping your sex at home will not only decomplicate your marriage, over the long haul it's much more fun to be good."

"Not Everybody's Doing It"

Some of the most sinister sounds drumming in Christian ears are variations of the theme, "Everybody's doing it." And whenever we hear these, we need to begin asking ourselves some questions:

1. Does this mean a half dozen of the world's populace, or millions? Two maybe? Could it be the echo of some one person reaching for justification?

2. What if everybody *is* doing it? As followers of the Lord we are called to live with an eye single to his glory. We do not take our standards from the world around us. Always our call comes from the Highest Source.

Adultery Still Remains Adultery

In vain we call old notions "fudge,"
And seek to bend our conscience to our dealing.
But yet the Ten Commandments will not budge
And stealing still remains but stealing.

So too for adultery.

Situational ethics is the name for that mind-pattern which adapts right and wrong to a set of special circumstances.

"Dear Dr. Shedd:

I am writing you because I am involved in something I never thought would happen. I direct the choir in our church, and as long as I can remember my relationship with the Lord has been the most important thing in my life.

A year ago I started taking violin lessons and I hesitate to put on paper what happened, but I do need help desperately. My violin teacher is a real genius, thirty years older than I am and a fascinating personality. He is everything I have always thought a master musician should be.

Well, almost before I knew it, we were sexually involved and this has been going on for several months. Many times I have promised the Lord it would never happen again, but every time we're together, it does.

What I can't understand is that I do love my husband and we have always had a good relationship. As a matter of fact, we still do.

But I must say that when I am with my music teacher, this has some beautiful aspects too. And even though I feel so guilty, I think I would just die if I had to give it up.

What I would like to know is whether there is any time, any way, in any stretch of the imagination that something like this could be right. They did it in the Bible, didn't they?"

Yes, they did it in the Bible. Sometimes it led to big trouble; sometimes it was part of the life style. But always the Christian measures his behavior against the teachings of Jesus. Our mail is piled high with letters from those who are looking for some small gap in the standards for Christian behavior.

There are none.

God put us together like this: In every sexual encounter we give a little of ourselves, leave a little of ourselves. Sex, for the spiritually sensitive, is too deep, too meaningful, too all-encompassing to scatter. This belongs exclusively to our partner. It is not ours to share elsewhere.

You say, "A part of me would just die if I had to give this up." That's exactly how Jesus said we would feel sometimes in going his way. Often following him may lead us up the hill to our own Calvary. And this is the amazing fact: *True joy comes from obedience*. The Bible says that he "for the joy that was set before him endured the cross" (Heb. 12:2).

Absolute fidelity in marriage may not always be exactly what we want, but New Testament Christians know without equivocation it is always what the Lord wants.

Fidelity Is More Than Sexual Faithfulness

For us fidelity has much broader connotations than absolute sexual loyalty. In the best relationships there will be a fidelity of sharing. We pledge ourselves to travel the inner roads together. We will take off our masks, come out from behind our façades. We will be honest with each other. But what we say *to* each other isn't the only kind of verbal fidelity either.

We also commit ourselves to faithfulness in what we say *about* each other.

Recently I had occasion to call a builder. We needed a builder, and he had been recommended. Since he doesn't have an office, I called him at home, and his wife answered.

Press agent supreme! "My husband is the best builder for miles around, mister; he's thorough; he's honest; he does what he says he'll do. He keeps very close check on everything and you couldn't do better anywhere."

Then on and on with accolades too numerous to mention.

When I did meet the builder, I told him what his wife had said. He grinned his million-dollar grin and answered, "Yeah, she's my number-one fan."

Do you have friends who put each other down when they are with you? They verbalize pot shots at each other and the whole party goes "Ho hum."

Some of these bores need nothing so bad as a pledge of verbal fidelity beyond their own front door. Do we really live by that Scripture which says:

"A word fitly spoken is like
apples of gold
in pictures of silver" (Prov. 25:11)?

So fidelity is of many kinds, but above all other kinds of fidelity the Christian couple who want the best will commit themselves to faithfulness in prayer; to meditation; to regular study of Scripture: to anything which tunes their marriage to divine love.

III

LORD, give us the courage to be transparent,
and the grace to make it possible.
we want to open up,
to share the hidden places,
to know and be known.

To Know and Be Known

Great marriage is letting each other into the deep places. It is for opening doors which may have been closed a long time; or secret doors where we have been slipping in and out. Great marriage is saying, "Let's look in here *together*. Come, let us begin to share the fears, the hurts, the shame, the good things too."

> "Lord, help us find those places in us which we have never opened to your love. Show us the subterranean chambers we have forgotten, the dark rooms where some small part of us is hiding. These too we hope to share—the musty and the moldy, the decayed and rancid. Cleanse us that we might more fully uncover all of us, known and unknown. Beginning now, lead us toward a total relationship with each other and with you."

"Why would my husband leave me for this little snip of a blonde? We've been married almost thirty years and I just can't understand it."

Like a steady crying we hear the somber lament of women who have been left when their husbands walked away. And in the mail the same low moan.

47

Sometimes it's a redhead, sometimes a brunette. Sometimes she's younger, sometimes older.

In this particular case we know the woman asking, "Why would my husband leave me for this little snip of a blonde?" We also know her husband's feelings: "Really, it's not what my wife thinks. She thinks it's all sex. So why does this girl matter so much to me? I'll tell you. It's because we can talk. I mean about anything. We communicate all the way. I can't tell you how good it feels to have one place in the world where it's absolutely O.K. to be who I am."

Most wandering men would rather have their "knowing" place at home. And the same for most women.

Fact: Heaven on earth is a relationship where two can say, "I want to know you. I want you to know me. Let us begin *learning* who we are, *sharing* who we are, no reservations."

"Tell Me What It Was Like When You Were a Kid"

"Were you happy? Sad? Full of fun? Fearful?"

We know a couple who met in the bath tub, but it wasn't as risqué as it sounds. Their mothers were best friends, they lived near each other, and spent considerable time together. And that's how it happened Liz and Mike met in the bath tub. They were bathed together as babies.

When they were six, their families moved. So Mike and Liz hardly crossed paths again till college days. Then they fell in love and married.

Most married couples did not know each other when they were little, and it isn't true that everything needs psyching back to the beginning. But some things do, and for us one little question has made a big difference: "Tell me what it was like when you were a kid."

There is a school of modern psychology which says, "Forget the past." Good advice for some people, and for all of us some of the time. It *is* possible to spend so long slogging around in the swamps of yesterday that we never get our feet on higher ground. We can overanalyze, over-psych, overdo in our personal histories. Yet a blanket application of "forget the past" is no panacea either.

Some of our hangups from yesterday *are* hanging us up from full sharing, full response. Going back together to search these out, to locate, to understand, to share together may be exactly what we need for inner freedom.

The Internal Society

A psychologist friend writes often about "the internal society." When we ask him what he means, he says, "I mean the whole range of influences in your past. Parents, grandparents, aunts, uncles, cousins, teachers, ministers, friends, neighbors, casual acquaintances and the well known; good-people memories, and bad. All these make up our internal society. We are all of us a conglomerate of variant input."

He says it well, and because we are the product of all this coming and going in and out of our minds, that makes us more interesting. Any couple willing to share, could probably go on forever uncovering mysteries, seeing new beauties, developing new sympathies, understanding why we are what we are. Any husband and wife committed to traveling these inner roads of total disclosure could say with meaning, "There is no person in the world more interesting than the person I married."

49

In addition to the request: "Tell me what it was like when you were a kid," there is another major in our marriage. This is the simple little query: "What's going on inside today?"

Over our years together we have learned to choose time and occasion for its asking. We never push. Some days it takes all the strength a person has just to go on breathing. But when we are ready, the question brings with it an excitement. We are free to move into the back rooms, down to the basement, up to the attic, wherever we need to go for more complete understanding.

This is scary. There is something in each of us which hesitates at the border of self-revelation. If I show you who I am and you don't like what you see, what do I have left? Nothing.

Grace

Because this fear of self-revelation is a very human tendency, there is one basic requirement for opening up to each other. "Grace" is a theological word which stands for "the free unmerited love and favor of God."

Jesus came to tell us many things, but among the amazing things he said, is any more amazing than this? "No matter where we have been, what we have done, nor how far the country we have gone to—

GOD LOVES US ANYWAY."

This is grace. And the more we can bring this attitude of Divine Grace into our marriage, the more completely we will be able to share.

"Do you have memories which make you nervous? Recollections about some awful part of you? You can tell me these if you'd like and I'll only love you more, because I'll know you better."

Grace enables us to share another thing:

"Could it possibly be that some of my far-out ideas might be worked into things worthwhile?

I have this dream about me, see! I'm somebody special and doing things I can hardly believe. Fine things. Fun things. Great accomplishments. Let me tell you about my high hopes, goals I have never reached. And would you also like to know of the times when I was really proud of myself, bigger than anyone knows? Plus some of my thoughts are so beautiful they seem almost too far out to muse on, but would you muse with me?"

So sharing our negatives is only a part of total knowing. The more we share those negatives, the more we uncover the "fine" in us. "This too we are. Beautiful! Let us now be grander together than we had ever dreamed."

What does all this have to do with sex? For us the answer is: Everything! Wise couples know that foreplay is much more than physical stimulation. Foreplay is also talk, talk, talk. Visit, visit, visit. Communicate, communicate. At the kitchen table, in the living room, riding together in the car, wherever circuits are being cleared by conversation, these same circuits are also being cleared for a more exciting sex life.

Mutual Self-analysis

Mutual self-analysis is the term we use for the sharing of our internal societies. We thought we knew each other well when we walked down that aisle to say "I do." But because we came from widely divergent backgrounds, we soon began to build barricades, and we didn't like it. We were hiding more and more and this was strictly no good.

Most people do not need a psychiatrist, and we didn't. What we needed was a friend, a helper, and most people would say, "That's what I need."

So we began what we call our "mutual self-analysis." For even a few moments each day we would open the inner doors. Sometimes we would slam them again quickly. Then on other days we would dare to keep them open longer. One minute. Two.

Gradually little by little, year by year we have built our mutual self-analysis to its present commitment: fifteen minutes per day sharing what's going on inside each other. And through this sharing we have come to know that *true and loving analysis in marriage leads to true and loving synthesis.*

"Tell Us Where to Begin"

One of our favorite starting places has been the self-help literature. At first we read lighter material, surface things which probed only enough to give us glimpses of the inner goings on. From there we have moved to the psychological writings, and then to pure psychiatry.

Most of the time we do not read together. Since one of us is an early riser and the other a late night operator, we have our quiet times at different hours. We are reading the same book, same article, but individually. As we read we mark.

A *candle* means new light. This we had never noticed before; a fresh thought.

An *arrow* means, "This hits me where it hurts. I'm getting nervous, I need to talk."

A *question mark:* "I don't understand."

Sometimes one of us writes "me" in the column. We never write "him" or "her." In research this delicate we find it best to extend each other the dignity of self-discovery, and we also extend each other the dignity to decide what should be shared.

So *step one* in mutual self-analysis is the decision to open up, wanting to know and be known.

Step two: reading, researching, discovering by some method those places where we need help.*

Step three: Coming together for listening, sharing, telling it like it is.

Question: Isn't it all right for us to have some hiding places, a private depository of very private thoughts?

Answer: Of course it is. From infancy up all of us cherish the secret little places where no one else can go. So great lovers will not push. These doors are not for beating on. They are only to be opened from the inside. Yet in the great marriages always the movement is toward sharing what needs to be shared, letting each other in.

She's worried about her past.

"Dear Dr. Shedd:

Please can you help me? I don't know what to do. Doug and I are going to be engaged on my birthday and I love him more than anything. What worries me is that I am wondering how much you should tell each other, and is it all right not to tell some things?

---

* Those interested in experimenting with mutual self-analysis as described here will find endless help if they honestly want it. The newsstands are replete with magazines on psychology, mental health, self-improvement. Same for the book stores. Libraries too will turn up almost limitless resource material for any couple on the hunt. Also see discussion beginning on page 90.

I don't like to say it, but the truth is I am ashamed of what happened in junior high. I was very immature and so lonesome. If only I could begin over again. I have never said anything to Doug or anybody about this part of my life. I guess it's because I'm afraid. What if he wouldn't like me as much? I have thought about it and even tried sometimes to tell him. But I get so scared. Do I have to tell?

Love,
Elizabeth"

No, Elizabeth, you don't have to tell. Or at least not until you have asked yourself some very important questions about Doug, and about you, and the two of you together.

Is Doug the kind of person you would describe as merciful? Have you seen signs in him which would indicate a forgiving spirit? Is he tolerant of others, kind in the things he says about them? Does he recognize his own faults?

And are you the type who can be satisfied with something other than togetherness all the way? Are you one of those people who can accept forgiveness from God without going through another person?

A famous psychiatrist says, "No individual can know complete peace until he has surfaced himself totally to one other person." So he goes on to advise that any couple considering marriage should put it all out on the table right now.

We don't agree. In the first place we have known some good marriages where they didn't tell each other everything before they were married, or after. Then too in the best marriages, they understand that complete surfacing is a goal, a pilgrimage. Sometimes it's a fun trip, sometimes it isn't. Sometimes it's embarrassing, sometimes awful.*

Because this is true, the wise couple will develop a wise sense of timing. Certain things are not for sharing *now*. Some memories are for giving up by bits and pieces. These need encouragement, comment, carefully worded questions. Then there are those which should be received in silence with a caress and the spirit which says, "I don't care where you have been or what you have done. I love you for what you are now and for what we can be together."

Number One on the Agenda—Time Alone Together, Quality Time

We live in a world of interruption, annoyance, distraction of every kind. Doorbell; telephone; committee meeting; television; children sapping our attention. Traffic to maneuver through. Meals to plan, prepare, eat; then tables to clear and dishes to scrape. Now do it over again, three times daily, and one of these probably a major production. Salaries to earn, bills to pay, checks to write, books to balance. Tension and strain, pressure and push. "Charge on, the mail must go through."

So where is the room in this schedule for knowing and being known? How can we possibly find time to relate in all this chaos and confusion?

Answer: We can't. We never will "find" time for togetherness. We must make it. "Time alone together, quality time" must be written large at the top of our agenda. And no matter the intrusions, we must keep first things first.

---

* *How to Know If You're Really in Love*, Charlie W. Shedd, Sheed, Andrews & McMeel, 1978, page 41.

Those who have read our other books and heard our tapes,* know we've had a special thing going for thirty-nine years. This is our once-a-week date. Dinner usually, and then one of our favorite drives, a movie, play, ballet, symphony, ball game, shopping, a long walk.

Sometimes if we're scheduled full in the evenings, we make it a luncheon engagement, or breakfast. These are not times when we're invited out by someone or entertaining guests ourselves. These are "dates" in the old-fashioned sense where we read each other's souls or share what are fun times for us.

Most couples are busy these days, or if they aren't, they soon will be, and time together alone will take some doing. Early in our marriage we saw that we were losing touch. Important things were crowding out the more important which for us was our togetherness. That's when we said, "If we have to book each other for our own special brand of quality time weekly, that's what we'll do."

All of us have a tendency to operate under the delusion that some time soon or down the road, there will be blocks of time to take it easy, enjoy, love. But for almost everyone we know, it doesn't turn out that way. Three days from now or six months have their own pressures.

"Where have all the flowers gone?" is more than a sad song. It is the authentic account of actual marriages where real calendars have crushed the things which really matter.

---

* Charlie and Martha Shedd have two 12-cassette albums in which this and other related topics are discussed. *Fun Family Forum* combines the very best from the Shedds' popular conferences with teenagers, young marrieds, and parents. The *Good Times with the Bible* series contains over three years of recorded Bible studies, group discussion, and live question-and-answer sessions on a variety of family-related subjects. Both series are available from Word, Incorporated, Waco, Texas 76710.

We even go out for breakfast alone when we have house guests. A note on the plate of Danish rolls: "Whenever we have overnight company, we have a compact that we will go out for breakfast alone. Thanks for coming."

You couldn't do that? For you it would not be gracious hosting? Amazing fact: Not one guest has ever said a negative thing about our breakfast out alone. Instead almost always comes the wistful comment, "Why don't we do that?"

Why not?

"Seek . . . first the kingdom" is in no small part a seeking for deeper relationships, and for most of us this takes time. Specific time. Committed time. Fun time. Holy time.

> "Lord, more than anything else we want to stay in touch with each other and with you. Help us to control our schedule and not let our schedule control us."

Thursday Afternoon Matinee

"Thursday afternoon matinee" does not sound like anything super-special. But for Roy and Claudine it is.

Roy is a stockbroker with some control over his own schedule. Claudine keeps house, busies herself with raising four children, and she's crazy about Roy.

If you could see them together, you would know these two have a good thing going. Actually, they have a lot of good things going. But according to them, their "Thursday afternoon matinee" is one of their best things going.

On Thursday afternoon Roy comes home at one o'clock. After lunch together, they lock themselves in their den for "Thursday afternoon matinee." Let the phone ring, or doorbell, these two are alone for three hours. They read, talk, listen to records, and then in Roy's words, "We proceed to miscellaneous items on the agenda."

At four o'clock the children come home from school and life returns to normal at their address.

Whether we call it "Thursday afternoon matinee" or label it something else, we do a good thing when we say: "Somehow, some way we *will* spend time with each other celebrating."

Why all this talk about "time" in a book on sexual celebration?

A doctor friend of ours says:

"Sexual disfunctions are usually a symptom rather than a cause. Whenever the sex life is not what it should be, there has been a breakdown in communication."

Favorite Talking Places

We once asked a group of couples, "Where are your favorite talking places?"

Steve & Helen: "We do our best talking on the cellar steps. Do you know how that happened? One night when the kids were especially noisy, and we simply had to discuss something, we went to the cellar steps, closed the door, and we've been doing it ever since. For us there is something almost holy about our cellar steps."

John & Audrey: "We lie down together on our big shaggy den rug. That's when we communicate best. It's so soft down there. But that's not all, down there we get a different view of everything, and that helps."

Phyllis: "Newt was an 'all-everything' line backer and from watching him play, you would never guess that he's afraid of anything. But he is. Mostly he's afraid to talk. Except in bed he'll talk some. So I thought about this a while and I told him, 'Newt, before we have sex, we're going to talk. We're going to lie here and hold hands. I'm going to tell you what I'm thinking and you're going to tell me what you're thinking. You wouldn't believe the difference this has made. Do you suppose it's because he doesn't have to look at me? Or because he knows what's coming? Or because he's looking up, kind of like a person does in prayer? Anyway that's when we talk best."

Brad: "If you won't laugh, I'll tell you something that happened long ago in our marriage. We had clammed up completely, and I do mean completely. Sure, we talked about things we had to talk about—the budget, kids, activities, church, but even that was minimal. Then one time at the office when I was recording some directives to my salesmen, an idea hit me. There was something I had been wanting to tell Lydia. It was something she had done, and I was proud of her, but I just couldn't tell her. So I put in on cassette. She knows how to play the machine, because we use it together in our Sunday school class. Well, I left it beside the kitchen sink. You probably can guess what happened. She put a message on the cassette for me. You think that's strange? We do too now, because we have learned finally to open up some; and where it started was those cassettes."

Charlie & Martha: "We do our best talking on our rocking love seat. If we couldn't buy another, we wouldn't sell our love seat for a million dollars, or two."

Secret Language

Carl and Eleanor were active members in one of our churches. They were young, outgoing, compassionate, excellent parents, very much in tune with each other and with the Lord. Also exciting to know. One reason they were exciting is that they were born deaf mutes. They couldn't hear or talk. Then they went to special schools and learned the making of sounds so they could carry on a conversation, and could they ever read lips!

Like most husbands and wives we have our own secret phrases, words, and sentences. Sometimes when we're across the room from each other, we can talk with eye movements, lips and facial gestures. Now and then our conversation is important little bits of business, but most often love messages, including sex.

It's a fun thing for us, this silent communication in public. And for years without our knowing it, our silent communication had also been a fun thing for Carl and Eleanor. How do we know? Because at our farewell reception, with a gleam in their eyes, they said, "We're going to miss your little exchanges, particularly at the Wednesday night dinners." Of course, we went on to ask, "Did you understand *everything* we said?" "Yes," they answered, "almost everything, but we never breathed a word of it. And we just loved our Wednesday nights at the dinner, and afterward."

Then there are also secret little verbal exchanges which can be heard by anyone, but understood only by the *two of us*.

Mr. Mercer ran a small business, and I worked for him one summer between school years. This was a business where customers phoned in orders. But when his line was busy, some customers called his house. So his wife took those orders, and then she phoned them to the office.

For that reason he talked to her many times each day. And always he would end their conversation with these three letters: "C Y K."

Finally, when my curiosity got the best of me, I simply had to ask him: "What's with the 'C Y K,' Mr. Mercer? I notice you never use it except when you close a conversation with your wife."

"Well, I guess not," he laughed. "Those three letters mean 'Consider Yourself Kissed.' "

Then he went on to explain he didn't want to embarrass customers, but he did think married couples are smart to have some private little secrets.

They are.

Why Can't We Talk about Sex?

(From seminars in Aspen, Colorado; Knoxville, Tennessee; Jekyll Island, Georgia, come the following reports. Participants are couples, mostly young, who had remained after regular sessions to discuss the theme: "What We Wish Someone Had Told Us about Sex Before We Married.")

"Take Your Hand Off My Breast, Jimmy"

"It was a great day in our sex life when I could say, 'Take your hand off my breast, Jimmy, and scratch my back.' One of the things I wish we had known before we married is that it is O.K. to talk about sex while you're doing it. What you like and don't like, what your needs are at a given moment. For a long time we didn't do this, and do you know why? I think one reason is I was afraid to say anything to Jimmy, because he might think I was complaining about his love-making.

Then I decided that was silly, because he would get more out of it if I got more out of it. So I began talking and he did, and it was a whole lot better."

"You read a lot about foreplay as an important part of sex. If I could give some advice to young husbands, it would be, 'Slow down, boy, it won't go away. Whisper a few things in her ear. Things she likes to hear. Things you appreciate about her. Maybe something you've never told her before.' It honestly seems to me a man sort of warms up through his eyes, you know pictures in his head. But in our case, I think Louise warms up more through her ears. When I tell her how beautiful she is and what this means to me, that's what starts her going. Then after we're rocking along, I can still bring out more of her warmth by more warm words."

"When my wife first told me she wanted me to rub her back before we had sex, I was frankly a little offended and I couldn't figure out why. Then I decided it was a silly little twist in my thinking, because you see when you rub some- body's back, they turn their back to you. And I have always been overly sensitive to rejection. When I finally worked out what was bugging me, we talked about it and had a good laugh. Now it doesn't bother me any more at all. She really does have a beautiful back."

"When I was in college, I was the big jock, mostly basketball. And one of the things I liked best about it was the rub-down table. I happen to have calves that cramp when I'm tired and no way I can tell you how often I think back to those basketball rubdowns.

Well, I wish I had known sooner that it was O.K. to ask Marge to rub me before we had sex. Sounds stupid, doesn't it, but I kid you not, I thought she would think this was queer, so I didn't say anything. Then one time when my legs were really cramping bad, I did ask her to rub me, and she did. You know what came of that? You've heard about massage parlors? Well we have one. She rubs me and I rub her and we talk about where it feels best.

"I wish we had known earlier that you can also talk about what feels best in sex. I mean right at the time. 'Give me your feather touch .... Kiss me here .... Faster.' "

"For a long time right after we had sex, David would get up and go take a shower. The first time it happened, I wondered. Then when it kept happening, I began to feel insulted like I wasn't clean or something. So my inner response was one of hurt. But I kept still and I shouldn't have, because when I finally told him, he explained that his thoughts and feelings weren't like I interpreted them at all. For him it simply was a matter of physical comfort. You see, don't you, we went through a whole lot of unnecessary worry and hurt, because I didn't ask him why he did it. We have talked about honesty before sex and during sex. But I wish I had known it's O.K. to be honest after sex too."

This from a gynecologist:

"One reason we don't talk when we're making love is that we don't talk enough about sex when we aren't making love. Somewhere we've been taught that talking about sex is nasty, so we get verbally hung up over sexual words and sexual feelings. Well, my wife and I decided that even the sex terms which are terms of the street can be meaningful to us if we clean them up in our heads and use them only between us as a nice addition to our sex life."

Sad that so many four-letter
words have become "dirty."

"For Unlawful Carnal Knowledge"

But is anything dirty if we've cleaned it up together? Because someone else thought it vulgar, does it need to be vulgar with us? So many sex terms which are considered terms of the street today were not that in their origin.

In early America when people were arrested and placed in the stocks, their crime was written above them for all to see. "Stealing chickens"; "Bearing false witness"; "Unpaid debts"; plus a vast assortment of other misdemeanors. But those who were arrested for sexual carrying-on were labelled:

"For Unlawful Carnal Knowledge"

Shortened by the use of first letters only, this word came to be one of the most prevalent four-letter words for sexual intercourse.

Fact: Any language a couple uses together; any verbal interchange or sound, if it's a thing of beauty to them, it's a thing of beauty. The "dirty" is not in the word. It's in the head.

Knowing the Body

Jesus was a toucher.

"He stretched out his hand and touched (the leper)" (Matt. 8:3 rsv).

"He touched her hand, and the fever left her" (Matt. 8:15 rsv).

"And they were bringing small children to him, that he might touch them . . . . he took them in his arms and blessed them, laying his hands upon them" (Mark 10: 13, 16 rsv).

How many other times did he make physical contact with someone who needed the assurance of touch?

We once heard a masseur say that the skin of most adults is starved.

He's right. For a major part of our lifetime we may not have been touched as much as we should have been touched. The baby didn't get enough cuddling; the child didn't get enough hugging. The boy was told, "You better keep your hands off. People will think you're queer." The father was too busy to touch and the mother too preoccupied with other things. So the teenage girl gives in too quickly, because male hands turn her on. Or the father and son shake hands, because society says that's all men ought to do; shake hands.

We think every couple early in their marriage and frequently thereafter should lock their bedroom door, remove their clothes and lie on the bed for a caressing session. "Where do you like to be touched? Here? Lightly? Firmly?"

Experiment. Explore. Learn to know each other's bodies, the mysteries, wonders, responses.

How long should this go on? Twenty minutes? Thirty? An hour? Our answer is that it should go on for thirty-nine years and longer. Our bodies are marvels of Divine Creation in nerves and curves, tissues and fibers, bones, hair, muscles from the top of the head to the tip of the toes.

"Isn't it amazing how we are put together?"
(modern translation of Psalm 139:14)

The Uniqueness of You and Your Combination

"Dear Dr. and Mrs. Shedd:

We decided to write you, because we thought there might be some other couple who could do with some advice from us.

We've been married three years now and we're getting along real well, but at first it wasn't all that good.

66

Do you know what we finally decided? We decided we were paying too much attention to what other people said, including the experts. So we said to heck with it. They don't know what we need. They don't know what would make us happy. They don't know what we like. From now on we will just do our own thing.

You wouldn't believe how much better things have gone, like 100 percent better since we have tuned out all this expert advice and tuned in to our own feelings."

Well said.

Our union is unique. We are not competing with any other man or any other woman or with any other marriage. We are two unique and special people brought together by God who wants us to create something very special and unique.

We will let others worry about the statistical averages and the Madison Avenue surveys. We will pay less attention to what "they" say. Why should "they" impose boundaries on our relationship? They shouldn't. Our particular combination is different from every other combination and that isn't all the excitement either. Every day, every week, every year we're different. The two of us are different individually and together than we've ever been before. So right now is a new moment for new blending.

> "Thank you, Lord, for bringing us together for our own special celebration, *our* way."

"*To Know*"

There are thousands of biblical references to the word "know": "knowing, knowest, knoweth, knew." And they mean many things. But one of the scriptural meanings of the verb "to know" is a man and woman coming together in sexual intercourse.

Is the Lord trying to tell us something?

We think he is.

One more time great marriage is letting each other into the deep places:

To Know and Be Known.

IV

LORD, help us to break the patterns
   of our selfishness
      that we might focus more and more
      on each other's feelings,
         each other's needs.

Test for the "Otherness" Factor

1. Which words do I use most often? Check:
   "I" _____ "Me" _____ "My" _____ "Mine" _____
   "You" _____ "Yours" _____ "We" _____
   "Us" _____ "Our" _____ "Ours" _____

2. When we have a job to do together and it is not our favorite thing, but it has to be done:
   A. I always end up doing more than my share _____
   B. I leave most of it to my mate _____
   C. We divide it equally _____

3. Genuine gratitude is another characteristic of the unselfish. In the use of "thank you," or any expression which means the same, I rate myself:
   Excellent _____ Fair _____ Poor _____

4. When it comes to conversation and otherness, most of the time
   A. I am prone to tell what I think first _____
   B. I ask, "What do you think?" and wait for an answer _____

5. When things don't go my way in our marriage:
   A. I resent it _____
   B. I am a good sport _____
   C. I don't say much, I simply take it philosophically _____

71

D. I have a hard time cooperating _____

6. In doing more than is required such as complimenting, adding the small extras, happy surprises, I rate myself:
   A. Super _____
   B. A "now and then" person _____
   C. Near zero _____

"D" Love, "B" Love

"Dear Dr. and Mrs. Shedd:

I think I have finally discovered what is the matter with our marriage, and the matter is that my husband doesn't really love me. Oh, a little maybe, but most of the time I get the feeling he is loving himself loving me."

In every one of us there is this tendency to love for what we get out of it. We once heard a psychologist say there are two kinds of love: "D" love and "B" love. "D" stands for deficits. If we love someone with a "D" love only, then we are loving because of deficits in us.

"B" stands for being. When we love with "B" love, we love the other person for who they are. We are concentrating on them and we love them because they exist. Our major feeling for them is wanting to bless, not to use.

In every marriage there will be love of both kinds. Nothing is wrong with the feeling: "I love you because you are good for me. I like what you do for me, the way you make me feel." "I am a better person because of you than I would be without you." "You inspire me." "You give me stability." "You lead me to a deeper understanding of myself." "You make me feel secure." "I like the way I can lean on you when I need a place to lean."

"Without you I would not be what I am, and I am thankful."

In all these ways "D" love is a good thing.

But "B" love is better.

Always one requirement in the greatest marriage is a mutual attitude which says:

> "We love each other because God
> made us special
> We want to help each other be what
> God intended us to be,
> individually and together."

The wise couple knows this kind of attitude will not come special delivery tomorrow. The accomplishment of genuine "B" love is a lifetime goal.

Junior high girl: "You mean 'D' love is sort of like my cat. She doesn't rub against me because she likes me. She rubs against me, because it makes *her* feel good."

What difference does it make whether the predominance of our love is for self or the other person? In sex it can make all the difference as witness these quotes straight from where it's happening.

"We have four children, and my wife was nauseated for about seven months with each pregnancy. She tried all kinds of medication, all kinds of psychological gimmicks but nothing worked. Often for weeks at a time she could hardly function.

GRANT

Well, I guess you know what that would mean to a couple's sex life. It means there wasn't any. That's what it means. Months and months of abstinence and it was awful.

But we are very religious people and those wedding vows mean everything to both of us. Do you remember the phrase: 'For better or for worse?' I can't tell you how that helped me. Many times when I would get to feeling sorry for myself I would think back to that particular vow. You know so often we think only of ourselves, especially when it comes to sex, so I honestly worked at training myself to think of Ann and how she was feeling . . . what could I do to make it easier for her.

Now I'm not a saint and sometimes it was really tough going. But we made it and I will tell you something else about our sex life. We are making up for lost time now and I wonder if this is what the Bible means by that verse in Galatians 6:9, "In due season we shall reap, if we faint not."

MARY LOU

"Do you know what happened to me on our honeymoon? The very first night suddenly I was homesick and I began to cry. I realized I was leaving my family, the family I had grown up in. And I literally fell apart. What do you think David did? He took me in his arms and said, 'Go ahead and cry.' I think his understanding right then was the greatest preparation for sex any woman ever had."

74

"I do not get up to cook Bud's breakfast. I have a lot of friends who say I should be ashamed of this, but they do not know all of it. Bud doesn't eat breakfast and I just love to sleep in the morning. So he tells me not to feel guilty, but go ahead and sleep. Every morning before he leaves, he gives me a kiss on the cheek and this may sound strange, but even though I am sound asleep, I feel his kiss. And then somewhere inside I feel something special for a husband like Bud who lets me sleep and tells me not to feel guilty. This may sound even stranger, but I think that kiss on my cheek and those thoughts about Bud which I have in my sleep are a real sexual turn-on for me."

"It was a terrible shock to me the first time I couldn't make it. I thought it was gone forever. You know there are women who put men down at a time like that or make fun of them. Not my wife. I know one of the greatest things that ever happened in our sex life was her attitude right then. She didn't let on at all that she was worried. Instead she encouraged me, told me not to worry, and said it would come back. Thank God it did."

GLEN

"My husband is the sexiest man I know. And what does that mean? Lots of people think it means 'Handsome and well built'; you know, 'macho.' But Bruce isn't like that at all. He is short and kind of

POLLY

75

pudgy and wears thick glasses. So what makes him sexy? I will tell you. It is his patience.

You see my mother gave me the feeling that sex is a four-letter word, because she spelled it 'evil' or 'sick.' When Bruce realized what she had done to me, he didn't scold or put me down. He just began retraining me carefully and patiently. In my opinion it is things like this that make a man sexy, and if I could tell you about our sex life, I think you would know what I mean."

DIANE

"Walter travels and some weeks he is gone from Monday morning till Friday night. It has always been like that, and I want to tell you something that was a big surprise to me. Sometimes after a very hard trip, he didn't even want sex right away. He wanted to eat and rest and sleep. Well, I didn't feel that way, because I was always more than ready. So I was hurt and then when I was feeling sorry for myself, I even got suspicious and blew it up into something bigger than it ever should have been. Finally, I told him how I felt, and he explained the hard week he'd had and I could understand.

Then I prayed about it and the answer I got was that sex might be even more beautiful if I could quiet my own feelings and think about his. Anyway this is the idea the Lord gave me: think more about

76

Walter right now than about yourself. So I did, and it worked."

"If I had one piece of advice for young couples, it would be about the honeymoon. I would tell them that they would be smart to get separate rooms that first night, have a good rest, and then come together for sex.

JEAN

Honestly, when you think back, it really was something, wasn't it? All those parties; the plans; the reception line, standing there listening to people saying those inane things, because they couldn't think of anything else to say and you couldn't either. Then driving away with your dumb friends chasing you, and now you are supposed to climb into bed and make like Anthony and Cleopatra.

Well, here is something you may not believe. When we got to that motel room, I turned to Bob and said, 'I give you now the tiredest night of my life.' You know what he said? He said, 'I'm tired too. Good night.'

Looking back on it now, we laugh, but we both agree that was a good beginning."

SANDRA

"Do you know the term, 'de-personalizing a rebuff'? It is one of the things I learned when I was studying psychology at the university, and I think it can be applied to sex. For instance, I like sex early

77

in the morning before the children get up. And it was an insult to me when Tony didn't like it then.

At first I had these 'poor me' feelings. Then I thought about that, and the conclusion I came to was Tony doesn't like anything early in the morning except more sleep. Why don't you think of him as a great big bear just coming out of hibernation?

So I did, and that's what I believe they mean by 'depersonalizing a rebuff.' I think sex can be improved sometimes if you learn to do this."

"I have found that a little change of attitude can make all the difference. For instance, it used to really bother me when Charlie would come home from work and start playing around while I was getting dinner. My first reaction was, 'For crying out loud, Charlie, not now!'

MARTHA

So he would go away rejected and then I would feel guilty. This went on and on, and we were getting nowhere. I knew we were getting nowhere because he didn't quit approaching me at the kitchen sink and I didn't quit resenting it.

Then one night I decided to try something different. I turned and put my arms around him and said, 'Charlie, you're getting me so excited, I can hardly wait. See you in bed.'

Well, he went away and read the paper and instead of feeling negative toward each other, we were both looking forward. Isn't it strange what one little shift of attitude can do?"

GRETCHEN

"I think Eric must be the greatest lover ever, because when we have sex, he says his greatest pleasure is in giving me pleasure. Well, I know he really means it, so I do everything I can to give him pleasure, and then that pleases me."

"Our problem was that at first I thought of sex as an animal act. Then I read up on the differences between a male and female and learned that even though a man is thinking of sex as an animal act, his wife is thinking of it as a love scene. So I tried to think of sex as a love scene, and do you know what happened? The more I thought of it this way the more she began to think of it as an animal act. It really is amazing what happens when you start thinking about sex the way the other person thinks of it."

WOODY

ANNA MARIE

"When I got married, my grandmother told me, 'Don't worry about all this 50–50 stuff. If you will give yourself 100% and he will give 100%, you will have a 200% marriage.'"

"At first I used sex as a means of reward and punishment. I don't know where I got the idea but I have a vague recollection that it came from hearing my mother and her sister talk. But believe me that is a terrible thing to do, because when you do that, you are only being very selfish."

RUBY

Loving the Unlovable

What are the three most important words in marriage?
"I love you."
"I need you."
"Please forgive me."
Not bad, but here are three more which can make all the difference:

LOVING THE UNLOVABLE

Why do some couples make it through the tough places and others come undone? One answer may be that successful lovers have whatever it takes to return positive for negative.

Credo for the Rough Moments

"You've been snapping at me, rejecting me, but I want you to know that even when you aren't so lovable, I'm still loving the real you. You may be in a down mood and down on yourself, but I want you to know that even then I'm up on the basic you."
This kind of otherness requires rare control, but any-

one who has ever reached this high level knows that the view up here is worth whatever it takes.

We have found that "loving the unlovable" is followed by a big zoom in our sex life. Always.

Another Kind of Otherness—Sex Education

There is one type of sex education which supersedes all others. This is a father and mother who are so sexually happy that the children sense it.

Question: "Do you believe in demonstrating sex for your children?"

Answer: No way! To us the question seems ludicrous, but in our seminars it surfaces so often many parents must be wondering. And there are those in the mod and secular world who would say yes.

But most Christian couples will feel like we do. We want our children to know that sex is beautiful and that there are good things going on between mom and dad. Yet we also want them to know that this is holy business, sacred, and only for the two of us.

Question: "If we tell our children sex is beautiful, won't they be impelled to find out for themselves?"

Answer: The exact opposite is true. Children, teens, and adults flashing back, verify this fact: One of the most certain safeguards against second rate sex is feeling that things are first rate between mother and dad.

Small boy in family seminar:

Theme: When is your family happiest?

"My daddy is the happiest on Sunday afternoon when he comes out of the bedroom with my mother."

High school girl, sensing good thing:

She came home after school to find her dad sitting at the kitchen table. He'd been painting the house and now he was winding down another day's work. She joined him with a coke and they visited.

Through the window she caught a view of her mom on the ladder. Her parents were painting the house together. They had decided to do it this year on her dad's vacation. So the little woman was applying those last strokes on her section, and she was a sight. Old gray hat. Baggy pants. Shirt tail hanging out and every bit of her thoroughly splattered.

Kristy and her dad had always conversed well. Nothing heavy now, just plain fun talk. She chattered on about school, friends, plus miscellaneous. And all the while her dad kept glancing out the window. Suddenly, with a look she'd never recognized before, he said from deep inside, "Isn't mom beautiful?"

This is what Kristy says about that moment: "I will never get over the feeling I had right then. How my dad looked. That's when I first sensed something wonderful going on between my folks which I had never sensed before."

She's twenty-six, lovely to look at and very successful. She's the producer for a major television show.

Twenty-Six and Looking Forward

It was Valentine's month and we were being interviewed. The subject this particular day was love, sex, and marriage which always makes for a lively show.

When it was over, she took us into her office and said, "I want to tell you a story. When I was in sixth grade, one of my friends explained how babies were conceived. I couldn't believe it. Since my mother and I had an above average relationship, I went right home and told her what I had learned. Then I added, 'Mother, you didn't do that to have me, did you? You wouldn't!'

Do you know what she did? She threw up her arms, gave me her most ecstatic look, and rhapsodized, 'Oh yes, I did and it was *wonderful!* It *is* wonderful!'

I think that's one of the best things that ever happened to me."

What My Dad Told Me

"Before I got married, my dad said, 'Honey, I want you to know something about your mother. She's a sexy broad in the nicest kind of way.'

Well, that's sort of blunt, isn't it? But I got the message and I decided right there it would be one of my goals—to be a sexy broad in the nicest kind of way." (Husband sitting by her side in quiet voice: "Praise the Lord.")

Echoes from everywhere in the youth scene. "Why did they let me grow up in a vacuum? Don't they know we're going to get our information somewhere? Wouldn't it be better if they told it to us straight at home?"

It certainly would, but by our own survey, less than 5 percent of today's youth are getting the information they need.

Question: "Can we start too early?"

Answer: No. If we believe that sex is a gift of God, then we begin the day a child is born. By the time our children are ten or eleven, they should have a thorough presentation straight from us.

Rule: It is better to tell a child too much too soon than too little too late. If we give them all the facts in love and they have no need for it now, we can count on this: Our children come from their Creator equipped with an inside computer. What information they don't need yet, they will file for later. Then when the banal and bawdy come, they have a positive reserve for meeting it.

What makes a nervous child nervous?

Why is a confident child confident?

From what we've seen this is one answer: a solid sex education. Having learned at home that sexuality is a gift of God, a child is liberated. "These feelings I have are to be accepted, and what is even more important, they can become a beautiful part of my future."

> "My mom and dad are always fighting and yelling and saying stuff I don't want to hear. That is why I go over to Eddy's house a lot, because you can tell his mother and father

really treat each other nice—and when I'm around them, that makes me feel good."

So Christian witness is of many kinds, but is there any more important than this? That a child, a discouraged neighbor, a hurting friend, any observer wondering whether love is for real, might look at us and have this feeling:

"Then God created male and female
and behold, it was excellent
in every way."

Big "I" with Minus Mark

THE CROSS IS A BIG "I"
WITH A MINUS MARK THROUGH IT.

We don't know who said that first, but we first found it in a collection of ancient sayings on the Christian life. It apparently came from some perceptive saint in the middle ages, reflecting on these words of Jesus:

"If any man would come after me,
let him deny himself
and take up his cross daily
and follow me."

For the Christian there is such an awesome *every-day-ness* to the cross.

So what does the cross have to do with our sex life? Everything when we see the cross as a call to yield our selfish ways. Life is not for us first. It is first for relating properly to God, then to others, including the one other child of God we love most. And when we have learned to minus out our own selfish feelings, then our life is what it should be in every way, including sex.

V

LORD, *more than anything*
we want to be tuned in
to the source of real love,
to each other
and to you. Amen.

Christians Should Be Sexier Than Anyone

Where is the world's most exciting sex?

A national magazine seems bent on finding the answer. This particular "slick" advertises itself as the last word in sexual liberation. Explicit pictures and articles, ribald cartoons, find each issue straining to be more lurid than the last.

"The Sex Life of Our Major Cities" is one of their regular features. In this seemingly interminable series, the editors claim to take us where the action is.

Here are the best adult theaters. This way to the wide open night clubs. Over here for the actual stuff on stage, nothing simulated, the works. And don't go away, now down this alley for the kinky stuff.

Is this really the world's most exciting sex? Some of us know it isn't. These frenzied searchers for the "real" have never been in our bedroom.

Neither have they been in the bedrooms of men and women who know that sex at its best is a spiritual union between a man and a woman and the Lord.

So how do we make our bedroom the scene of "the world's most exciting sex"?

It should be clear by now that our answer is fine-tuning the spiritual life.

And how do we do that? Two answers:
1. By learning together from the Bible.
2. By prayer in duet.

"Seek Ye Out of the Book of the Lord" (Isa. 34:16)

"What difference could Bible study possibly make in our sex life?"

Answer: A mighty difference.

This is the word from two people who have been turning up the excitement for thirty-nine years: we make our bedroom the scene of the world's most exciting sex by fine-tuning the spiritual life.

The more we read our Bibles, ponder what we find there, share our insights, the closer we draw to each other in every way, including our celebration in the bedroom.

"Do you believe God speaks to you out of his Book? Do you believe that Bible study is one way to retrack your mind to its original dynamic?"

We do!

He speaks to us from other books and other places. From nature, happenings, friends, and events. But here between the pages of his Book, in a very special way, he speaks to us together.

In those early years when we began drifting apart, when we began hiding from each other, we decided this would not do for us. We must take some definite steps and one of these would be daily Bible study together.

"Together" for us did not mean what is often meant by reading together. Because there is an awesome gap in our metabolisms, we developed our Bible study to fit the wide spread in our timing.

We would read the same book, same passage, same verses, but we would read individually. And we would mark with those same special marks we use in self-analysis.

1. *Candle* for new thought: something we've never

seen before. This is exciting. Let's think it through together.

2. *Arrow* for a flaw: weakness in our thinking, touchy place, sin. This too we mark for sharing.

3. *Question mark:* "I don't quite understand this. Maybe you can help me."

Now with our marking done, we talk.

"I have a question. You have a candle. Teach me."

"I have an arrow here. Let me share the guilt I feel."

We never, absolutely never, put arrows applying to the other person. Always it goes better for us when we extend each other the dignity of noting our own shortcomings.

Sometimes we both have question marks at the same passage. Then we go on a hunt together.

Twenty times in thirty years we've been through the Bible using this method. The many different versions and translations on our shelves are for us more than a mere collection of Bibles. They are a registry of our growing oneness. And always the more we travel these scriptural roads together, the more we discover new roads to travel in our love.

Most couples come to their marriage from divergent theological backgrounds, but Bible study together can harmonize those backgrounds. And the results for those who stay with it will appear in every area, including the physical.

Prayer in Duet

Developing a turned-on, tuned-in prayer life is much easier talked about than done.

When we were first married, there were many awkward moments. But none more awkward than our initial attempts to pray with each other. "What if I told the Lord these things I am really thinking? If I said them out loud, would my husband understand?" "Would my wife think I was strange?"

To which comes a loud chorus, "We've felt that way too." Too scary, too familiar, too embarrassing.

Can this be the reason why less than 5 percent of the couples we know pray together with meaning?

Yet any Christian knows that the Bible sounds this steady beat: "Pray without ceasing" (1 Thess. 5:17); "Continue in prayer" (Col. 4:2).

So let's take another look. There must be a better way. And we found one: silent prayer.

We would hold hands, talk over the things we wanted to pray about, discuss our concerns.

Then we would pray silently.

Prediction:

> Any couple not now praying together
> Who will set aside a few moments each day
> To sit quietly, discuss their feelings, then
>   pray together silently;
> Any couple who will do this for thirty days
> Will experience improvement in every aspect of
>   their relationship
> And especially they will sense an exciting new
>   dimension in their sex life.

At a recent seminar we were approached early one morning by a beautiful little woman in her senior years, and this was her report:

"Remember last night when you talked about praying together silently? Well, I just must tell you what happened. My husband and I went home and talked about this. Then we had to admit that in forty-two years, except for blessings at meals, we had never really prayed together. We both love the Lord, we are both active in the church, but when it came to real prayer together, no.

"So before we went to bed, we sat there a long time and talked. We talked about the past, the future, and things we had never said. Then we prayed silently.

"Now here is what I want to tell you. For several months my husband has not been interested in sex and that has been a big disappointment to me. Well, this morning when we woke up, he was interested, and it was beautiful again. I thought maybe I should tell you my story, so that you could pass it on to others."

Tests for Spiritual Growth: "You're a Good Egg"

Most of us like to be called "a good egg." Your father and mother probably remember watching someone candle eggs at their grocery store. Your grandpa and grandma have seen it for sure.

The grocer would sit on a stool or stand behind the counter. Then he would take a small box with a hole on top, and inside a candle or a light bulb. Each egg from the farmer's wife would be carefully lifted and held over the hole to make certain this was a good egg. Against the light, bad eggs showed plainly.

Galatians 5:22 and 23 make up what we call the great egg candler of the Bible. By these verses we can test any teaching, any group, any movement, and the church. It's the same for us individually. And if we really want to know how we're doing in our marriage, the passage will candle that too.

"*The fruit of the spirit is love,*
joy, peace, longsuffering, gentleness,
goodness, faith, meekness,
temperance."

Important note:

The word is "fruit," not "fruits." Love, joy, peace, and all these good things are not the work of man, woman either. They are God's doings, not ours. They are by-products of our life with him. And because this is true, we need to be constantly checking.

Marriage for the Christian couple goes better when the relationship is held up often to the light of the Lord. For those who would like to "candle" their marriage by Galatians 5:22, 23, we present here nine test questions. The extra words included with each are selected from other translations or chosen because we believe they are an honest interpretation of the original.

–1–

"The fruit of the spirit is *love*."

Is there an increasing concern for each other in our marriage?

More and more do we really care what our mate thinks, feels?

Are we growing in our "otherness"?

More words for "love" which we have found in various versions or in our own translation:

charity . . . caring . . . concern . . .
solicitude . . . devotion.

"The fruit of the spirit is *joy*."
*Are there increasing seasons of gladness in our relation-
ship?*
Are there more times when we sense the glow of real
happiness; when we plain feel good together?

Other possibilities:
jubilance . . . cheerfulness . . .
elation . . . laughter . . . mirth.

–3–

"The fruit of the spirit is *peace*."
*Is there an increasing quiet in our hearts, in our home,
in our love?*
More and more are we truly content, relaxed?

Other possibilities:
serenity . . . composure . . .
harmony . . . repose . . .
tranquility . . . stillness.

–4–

"The fruit of the spirit is *longsuffering*."
Is there an increasing stretch in our attitudes?
Do the little oddities in each other and in all others
disturb us less?
Are we more patient? More even tempered?
Jesus stood for something, and we will. We do not

want to become so broad that we flatten out into "anything goes." But even when we must disagree, can we do so with a greater appreciation of the other person's rights?

Additional possibilities:
    forbearance . . . flexibility . . .
        tolerance . . . adaptability.

−5−

"The fruit of the spirit is *gentleness*."
Are we increasingly kind, more courteous, softer in our touch?
Physically, mentally, verbally, are we more tender?
Longsuffering deals with our attitude toward those things people do to us. This question asks the opposite: Are we more Christlike in the things we do to other people?

Added possibilities:
    docile . . . soothing . . . compassionate . . .
        mellow . . . gracious.

−6−

"The fruit of the spirit is *meekness*."
Is there a growing self-honesty in each of us?
From the many interpretations of meekness, we have worked out our own definition:
    "True meekness is to know the difference between what we are right now and what God intends us to be."

For us closing these gaps is one more achievement of
great marriage.

"Measure us, Lord. Keep measuring us."

Other possibilities:
mildness . . . humility . . .
yielding . . . resignation . . .
submission.

–7–

"The fruit of the spirit is *goodness*."
More and more do we seek to be a blessing?
Do we reach out to help, make an effort to do something good, say something kind, lift?
There is a goodness which counts itself good, because
it isn't bad. But Christian goodness is never inert. It doesn't
hold back in the face of need, nor hesitate to act for the
welfare of another.

Other possibilities:
ministry . . . helpfulness . . .
generosity . . . service.

–8–

"The fruit of the spirit is *faith*."
These fears of ours, are they on the decline?
Do we worry less, trust more?
Do we really believe there is a power greater than our
own?

When we are anxious, are we better able to share our anxieties with each other and trust the Lord?

> Additional possibilities:
>   reliance . . . belief . . .
>   confidence . . . assurance.

–9–

"The fruit of the spirit is *temperance*."
Are we more and more in charge of our emotions?
Are we growing in that kind of self-control which is truly Christ-control, poised with his poise?

The Bible says, "All coheres in him" (Col. 1:17, Moffatt). Do they? Are we cohering with his coherence?

If the Spirit of the Lord is really at work in us, we should rattle less, scatter less, crater less. Is this how it is with us?

> Other possibilities:
>   self-restraint . . . self-rule . . .
>   self-mastery . . . self-discipline.

Anyone pondering these test questions seriously will realize that great marriage does not come by the lucky matching of two horoscopes. Touching the deeper levels, the higher regions are reached only from a lifetime of tuning to the Lord, uniting our two lives with him.

And since God is love, the more we tune in to the divine wave length, the more our love becomes divine.

For us this is what the sex act is all about. The two of

98

us together seek divine harmony, oneness with the primal force of his creation.

And when we touch it, then we know why "God created male and female," and we can say:

"Excellent in every way."

QUESTIONS

ANSWERS

COMMENTS

Questions, Answers, Comments

Questions, questions, thousands of questions. They come in the consultation room, they come by mail, and they come at seminars, retreats, workshops, and forums. Whenever we conduct a public session on marriage, we follow it with a period for dialogue. Participants may write any question anonymously.

A panel is appointed to sort the questions into groups and from there, we take off.

BECOME ONE?

Question: The Bible says we are to become one. Exactly what does that mean?

Answer: Because the original usage is a bit vague, no-one knows exactly what it means. Perhaps the Lord wants each couple to work out for themselves what it means for them. For us it means absolute fidelity in many ways, one of which is sex.

We like to think of "oneness" as "one unit."

Why Would He?

Question: Can you tell me why my husband would have an affair? He has always told me I was the best. I honestly don't see how it could be any better. Yet recently when I became suspicious, he admitted what he had done. Talk about a put-down, I simply can't understand it. Why?

Answer: Psychiatrists tell us sometimes a man can be very happy at home and still have an affair, because of things in his past. So maybe the answer to your "why" is far back there before you ever knew him.

Yet we must be careful with this kind of reasoning. We accomplish nothing if we say, "It's in his sub-conscious," or "Something must have happened in her past." Most marital problems are only corrected when we begin at the mirror. But when we have done that and have honestly asked the Lord to show us our faults, then we do well to say, "Maybe I shouldn't take this so personally."

In this case if the husband is honestly sorry and wants to understand what makes him unfaithful, he can find help. Almost anywhere we live these days, there is someone not too far removed who can guide us to the negatives in our history.

Unless the unfaithful husband does this, chances are that his behavior will repeat itself. And here it is again—the Christian couple will make a commitment to absolute fidelity. Then having done that, they will do everything possible to put themselves in condition for faithfulness.

Fornication

Question: I don't think my husband has ever been unfaithful. But I wonder sometimes if he isn't leading up to something. I don't think I am imagining anything here, because he works in a textile company with a lot of unmarried girls. I know some of them are very attractive to him.

Anyhow lately he has been giving me the argument that "adultery" is sex outside of marriage with another married person, and he says that's what the Ten Commandments forbid. But "fornication," he says, is sex with someone who isn't married and it's not the same thing.

Can you give me some guidance?

Answer: No one would believe how often the "fornication" or "adultery" questions surface in our mail or in our seminars. All scholars hold that the Bible strictly forbids fornication in the same way it forbids adultery. Many say there is so little difference in biblical usage that the words are almost interchangeable.

We don't think you are being overly suspicious, because we know other husbands who went through this same routine. The human mind has a tendency to look for gaps in every hedge, cracks in every wall.

But of this you can be sure. The male mind rationalizing sexual possibilities is not the highest source of biblical scholarship.

Submit Completely?

Question: I can't tell you the number of times I've heard our minister preach from Ephesians on wives submitting to their husbands. It bothers me and I'm not the only woman in our congregation who feels this way. To be a Christian does a wife have to let her husband have his way in everything, including sex? What if we don't feel like it sometimes, or don't enjoy certain things? Can you help us?

Answer: Some of the things we hear in religious circles bother us too. And one of these is the out-of-context quotation, "Wives, submit yourselves unto your own husbands" (Eph. 5:22). To understand it in context is to know that Ephesians 5:21 says, "Be subject one to another, out of reverence for Christ" (RSV).

In its original, the meaning is that we are to listen to each other, yield to each other, cooperate with each other. Then in addition we are to listen together, yield together, cooperate together with the Lord.

We also believe that "submit" in biblical terminology clearly includes the husband submitting to the wife sometimes and both submitting to the Lord, individually and together.

Always for us the Christian relationship includes this sacred concept: "There is something more important than that you should please me: this is that you should be true to the Divine in you and that together we make it our aim to please the Lord."

MUTUAL ORGASM

Question: We read so much about the importance of mutual orgasm that we are getting confused. My husband and I have what we think is a marvelous sex life. But most of the time we do not climax together. And sometimes I don't at all, but I enjoy it very much. Then when I feel the urge he makes sure my pleasure is complete too. Now why does mutual orgasm matter? Do these people who write such things really know what they are talking about?

Answer: No, they don't know what they're talking about *for you*.

Christian couples celebrating in their bedroom should not strain to reach someone else's idea of perfection. If you could talk to some of the couples we talk to, you would know how right you are when you call your sex life marvelous.

TROUBLE CLIMAXING?

Question: My problem is that I have trouble climaxing. Sometimes I do, but even then it seems to take forever until we are both almost worn out. What can I do?

Answer: Because this question comes often, we asked for some input at one of our recent seminars. Amazing how many women empathized with thoughts like this:

"What helps me most is concentrating while we are having sex. With me this is no time to let my mind wander"; "My biggest help is thanking God for my husband wanting me."

But most of the wives said, "She should go to a doctor. If her problem is physical, he can help her. If it's in her head, like most doctors believe, then she'll need another kind of help."

A Rush Job

Question: Everything my husband does is a rush job, including sex. That's not good for me, because I respond better with considerable foreplay and a slow warm-up. How can I get him to take it easy?

Answer: We don't know any other answer than communication. You have every right to insist that he calm his "charge-on" tendency long enough to get you ready. And here's a thought which you might ask him to ponder. We have a Frenchman friend who says, "It is better to make love once a week for five hours than five times a week for one hour."

We think he's a bit addled but what he's trying to say is very important for some people, including your husband.

Birth Control

Question: My wife has this hang-up about birth control. I mean about not using any. I'm not sure where she got it, because our church doesn't forbid it. But she says, "If the Lord doesn't want us to have a baby, we won't." She admits it would not be good for her to get pregnant now for a lot of reasons. I can't prove it, but I honestly think she isn't at her best sexually because she has this lurking fear of pregnancy. Do you know anything I can do to change her mind?

Answer: Yes, one thing you can do is to get her to focus on the concept that sex is for much more than having children. This is God's gift for celebrating the love relationship. We think if you have not done so, you could bear down on the fact that both of you need sex without fear early in your marriage. All of us come into marriage with a reservoir of frustration which needs emptying before we can be at our best every way, including parenthood.

HARDLY EVER

Question: My husband isn't impotent, but the problem is he is hardly ever interested. I mean like once a month or less. Even on our honeymoon all he wanted to do was play tennis. I can't understand it, because he was a super athlete in college. He is a nut about his body. He jogs, works out with weights and keeps himself in perfect condition. When I complain that I am sexually lonesome, he will say he is the normal one and he makes me feel evil.

If I suggest we need help, he absolutely refuses to discuss it with me or anyone. For years I've tried everything I know, and of course, I have prayed. I've even thought of leaving him. I know I'm attractive to other men. What can I do with this man?

Answer: Probably nothing. Even God cannot help those who refuse help. Any decision you make will have to be based on that fact. Sounds desolate, doesn't it? And it is. But the truth is you are much more normal than he is.

IMPOTENCE

Question: My husband has been losing interest in sex and lately it is almost nil. I don't like this, because sex has always meant a great deal to me. He makes fun of me when I let him know I need him. He says I'm oversexed and most men lose interest after fifty. Is this true? It bothers me very much and I honestly don't know what I'm going to do. Can you help us?

Answer: It is not true that most men lose interest after fifty. But impotence is a common problem and there are some important things to remember here. Many men experience temporary impotence when they are under strain, overworked, going through stress, unduly worried. But if it continues, the next move is to the doctor's office. Sometimes the husband can be helped medically. Sometimes it is a psychological problem and he will need help probing certain factors in the mind. We are often asked, "How long should we let this go on before we start worrying?" One doctor says, "Don't let it go past thirty days." And all doctors say, "The sooner it gets to us, the more likely the recovery."

Here is one more reason why it is important for a couple to develop a totally honest communication. With problems like impotency, the sooner faced the better. And it goes without saying, the Christian wife will be kind, encouraging, patient and nonscorning.

FREE-FLOATING FANTASY

Question: What bothers me is some of the thoughts I have while we are having sex. They are only flashes, but very real. Does everybody have these flash thoughts and is this wrong?

Answer: Yes, every honest person we know admits to flash thoughts of others during intercourse. We don't think this is wrong provided it can be controlled and the mind brought back where it belongs, namely to the beauty of *our* sexual union.

For any couple honestly wanting to help each other with fantasy, here is one possibility: "Let's try for a time letting our minds go while we're having intercourse. Since we can't control each other's thoughts anyway, we will extend each other the right of free-floating fantasy. Then at the moment of climax we'll bring our minds into focus on each other and praise God."

Prediction: Any couple who will practice this high level of honesty will:

    A. Be much more relaxed about themselves and their sexual relationship;

    B. Enjoy the sexual experience in a new freedom;

    C. Find their minds wandering less and less to focus more and more on their own celebration.

MORE ON LUST

Question: It really bothers me when I read Jesus' words, "Whoever looks on a woman and lusts after her has already committed adultery in his heart." That means I have committed adultery many times, but I don't want to. Am I quoting this correctly?

Answer: Yes, you are quoting correctly, and most men have felt like you. Many women, too, look at men and lust after them.

Those three words, "in the heart," are all important. Several scholars we know point out that committing adultery in the heart is decidedly different from committing adultery in bodily act.

For us there is also a sharp distinction between committing adultery *in the mind* and committing it *in the heart.* Flash thoughts, sudden fantasies, human urges are a real threat if we let them go from the mind to the heart.

But the main solution is to be honest with God. If we tell him we have these thoughts; tell him we want to be what he wants us to be; yield them immediately to him; he assures us that he understands. He forgives.

> "If we confess our sins,
> he is faithful and just
> to forgive our sins
> and to cleanse us
> from all unrighteousness"
> (1 John 1:9).

THE BELLY DANCER

Question: I need help with a problem which may be unusual, but it is important to me. When we go out, my husband wants me to dress in a way that embarrasses me. Do you know what I mean? Low necklines, slit skirts, things like that.

I can't understand this. He says it would mean something to him for other men to notice me that way. Do you know anyone else who has ever had this same problem and what did they do about it?

Answer: Yes, this problem surfaces often and what women do about it varies all the way from cooperating to saying an absolute no. We think you need to be true to yourself, and your husband needs to reorient his mind in the direction of reality.

What he doesn't know is that "come-on" girls who throw it around may be nothing more than "come-on girls" throwing it around.

Some time ago the headlines were making a great hullabaloo about an American millionaire who had married some Egyptian belly dancer. The gang was discussing this in the barbershop as they are prone to do, when the old barber droned, "If he wants what I think he wants, he should have married some country girl from Iowa!"

Vibrators Too?

Questions:

From a worried wife: "My husband is a barber and one time he brought home a vibrator, because I had muscle spasms in my back. Well, you can imagine what happened. Not only was it good for muscle spasms, but the sensation was so soothing and pleasant, I asked him to rub me all over. He did, and I almost went crazy. So that got him excited, and we had one of the most fantastic experiences I'm sure anyone ever had. But here is the problem. We kept on doing it until it has become a regular part of our love-making now. Is this all right? You can see it kind of worries us."

From a husband wondering: "My wife has always been very slow to respond sexually. Recently I saw an ad in a magazine for a vibrator. I sent away for it and I must say it's helped her considerably. I also like for her to use it on me sometimes. Then we got into an unusual discussion with out study group at the church and it was about different kinds of sex. How it all started I don't remember, but it did give me an opportunity. I casually introduced the vibrator subject and the minister's wife said, 'Don't you think if God intended us to use vibrators he would have equipped us with them?' Actually she is kind of pious about everything, but what she said still bothers us somehow. Do you know other people who use vibrators and should we worry about it?"

Answer: Yes, we know couples who use vibrators and we think it is much too simplistic to hold that we should only use those things which are part of our original creation. We wear clothes, don't we? We drive cars, live in houses, watch television.

A vibrator not only adds pleasure at certain times, it can also be the difference between fulfillment and frustration. Some couples we know used one for a while and then they outgrew it. Others find it a nice part of ongoing sex.

Say it again—Anything not physically or emotionally damaging; anything not forbidden in the Bible can be "excellent in every way."

Suggestion: Have you considered buying your pastor and his wife a vibrator for Christmas?

This Too?

Question: "What do you think about anal intercourse? Is this all right, too? When my husband first talked about it, I was horrified. I'd never heard of such a thing. Then we discussed it and finally you probably know what happened. We recently read in a book that this is what the Bible means by sodomy. We are Christians and we don't know anyone else we can talk to about this, because we would be embarrassed to discuss it. Even with our doctor we hesitate to bring it up."

Answer: This subject surfaces in Christian circles, and because we have had no personal experience with it, we have consulted doctors for their answers. They tell us there is high incidence of bacterial infection in this practice.

Bible scholars disagree on the definition of sodomy. A few might say it includes anal intercourse, but most believe it deals exclusively with homosexuality.

Conclusion: Say it again—When the Bible is not specific, it is up to each of us to decide before God what is right for us.

WINDOW PEEPING

Question: "The most terrible thing has happened. My husband was picked up by the police for window peeping. There has been a lot of talk in our neighborhood about a peeping Tom and I never would have believed it: Why does a man do this?"

Answer: To some questions there are no pat answers. We aren't the ones to help with this problem except to say you must understand your husband does need help. He needs help from a psychiatrist. It is almost certain that the causes for behavior like this lie deep in his subconscious.

Married couples often ask us about other behavior variances which need more help than we can give them. Here are some of those which do need prompt attention from psychiatrists, psychologists, or professional counselors—sadism, masochism, voyeurism (*the peeping Tom*), fetishism, homosexuality, lesbianism, exhibitionism, nymphomania, transvestism.

Other problems also come our way which should be

presented to the medical doctor. These include drugs and sex; sexual depressants; sexual stimulants; premature ejaculation; frigidity; alcoholic problems; venereal disease; menstrual complications.

PORNOGRAPHY

Question: "This week I had the shock of my life when I found an old suitcase back in one of our closets jammed full of the cheapest kind of magazines and books. Some of them were the type you might see at newsstands, but others I can hardly believe, they are so vulgar. Then in a pocket of this suitcase I found some pictures and stories in my husband's handwriting and they are just awful. I know he even drew some of the pictures. What shocks me is that I have always thought we had a good sex life. Can you tell me why a man would keep a collection of things like this? He is a deacon in our church and teaches Sunday school and I know he is sincere. So why?"

Answer: There are many reasons why a man is interested in pornography and most of the answers are to be found somewhere in his history. This is another place where you should "depersonalize" your reaction and recognize that he needs help. You can help by bringing it out in the open. Discuss it with him. Let him talk. Perhaps he needs the expertise of a professional, and he should be encouraged to seek it. Although a part of him gets a prurient satisfaction from these things, it must be a heavy load, too, for a Christian to live with this in his mind and on his heart. Meanwhile keep loving him, keep your sex life active, keep him talking.

Quarreling for Sex?

"My husband and I caught on to something recently we want to share.

We love each other very much, but we are both strong-willed, so we have many disagreements, some of them intense. Sooner or later we make up and one way we make up is to have sex. Then we discovered that sex always seemed extra good after a fight. So what difference does that make?

Well, when we got it out in the open, we had to admit we might actually start a fight because of what happened afterward. So the conclusion we came to is that good sex has to be for good reasons. Building up unnecessary tensions and baiting each other; saying things we don't really mean can be dangerous; and over the long run that is not the best way to have the best sex life."

Change of Life

Question: "Isn't all this stuff about change of life mostly foolishness? I get so tired of my wife using it as an excuse for everything, and especially for cutting down our sex life. I feel like telling her, 'Come off it, you're not the first to go through menopause.' "

Answer: We think you need to change your attitude. For some women the change of life is real trauma. What a woman needs now is not a man who says, "Come off it," but a husband who will give her tender, loving care. Why don't you try that for a while and see what happens?

But you are right that menopause doesn't need to cut

down on sex. Some women even become more passionate during these years. Yet in every situation we know where the wife has warmed up with menopause, there is a husband who has been stepping up his tender loving care to meet her rough times.

Male Menopause?

Question: "Do men go through a change of life too? I wish I knew. Some of the things we read say they don't, but something has sure happened to my husband sexually, and in other ways."

Answer: Ask ten doctors whether men go through menopause and there may be ten different answers. Yet some men do go through periods when they change behavior. When this happens, they might need physical examination and medical attention. But always this is a fact: the loving concern of a caring wife is an important part of the basic treatment.

Early Hysterectomy

Question: "My doctor says that sooner or later I must have a hysterectomy and he recommends I do it before too long. He is a member of our church, a good friend of ours, and I trust his judgment, but I am wondering. The reason I am wondering is that my best friend had a hysterectomy and she says it almost ruined their sex life. I happen to know she and her husband have had a hard time even when things are normal.

My husband says, 'Don't worry. I'm a great lover. I

know a lot more about women than Maudie's husband.' (Maudie is the best friend I was telling you about.)

This business about my husband being a great lover is sort of a joke between us, but he really is. I feel sure that would make some difference, but what do you think?"

Answer: What we think is that your husband is right on target. His love can make all the difference in every way.

No CHILDREN?

Question: "This is something we wouldn't want to tell anyone else, but we finally decided to share our thinking with you to see if we are way off. We have been married eight years and first we took it for granted that we would have a family some day. Both of us work at good jobs which we enjoy. People ask (especially our parents) when we are going to have children. This has bothered us, but lately we have been discussing it and we were almost shocked when we both admitted that one reason we don't want children is because we like sex so much.

Is this being selfish? Does everybody in the world have to produce?"

Answer: No, everybody doesn't have to produce. We don't think you should be uptight about your attitude. The Bible does say, "Be fruitful and multiply." But there were also people in Bible times and there have been many since who did not and do not have children, yet have lived fruitful lives. And aren't there many ways to "multiply" our influence besides having children?

We are glad your sex life means so much to you. And

we can imagine that "Male and female, excellent every way" could mean without children for some.

But you should also know that sex can be "excellent in every way" with children.

Cleanliness

Question: "My husband and I are growing apart fast. This may sound silly, but the main problem is that he won't keep clean. He says I make too much of it. But honest, sometimes I can hardly stand him near me. And his lack of personal cleanliness has almost ruined our sex life. What can I do?"

Answer: We don't know any nifty tricks except maybe inviting him into the shower with you. Some people find sex in the shower, or at least foreplay in the shower, exciting.

Have you considered the fact that your husband may have a hang-up which goes way back in his history? If he does, he might need counseling.

But you have a right to insist that he clean up his act. Again: sex is not excellent in every way if it includes something physically or emotionally damaging. Obviously your husband's failure to keep clean classifies as "physically and emotionally damaging."

He's Turning Her Off

Question: "My husband says I am getting frigid, and this hurts me, because I have never been that way. I am a

Christian and even though some of my friends seem to think sex is questionable, I have always enjoyed it. I believe God meant it to be good. However, my husband is right that our sexual relationship is not what it used to be. And the problem is he seems to turn me off by all his beer drinking.

As soon as he gets home from work, he starts drinking and after dinner, it's back to his beer. Then he gets sleepy and drifts off watching television. When I wake him and tell him it's bedtime, he wants sex. Sometimes I can hardly stand him, because honest he smells like a brewery. Don't tell me we should have sex before he begins drinking. We have three children. What can I do?"

Answer: Your options are limited. You can tell him you don't like it which you have probably already done many times.

You can refuse to have sex when he is in this condition which may be the most effective curative, but as you know that has other dangers.

If your husband will go with you, you should find professional help. He needs to know why he drinks to the point of repulsing you. Is it something in his background? Is it simply a destructive habit? Or is it plain selfishness? Whatever it is, the problem must be resolved.

We strongly urge you to seek out a minister or a counselor who can guide you wisely.

Too Fat

Question: "When my husband and I were first married, we had a great sex life. But lately he hasn't been so interested. When I asked him what was the matter, he really shocked me by telling me that I was too fat. Do you think this is fair?

So I am forty pounds overweight. Well, a lot of women are. I have tried, but when I lose a few pounds, I start eating again and a lot of the time I gain back even more. I need help. What can I do? It would be so much easier if he would help me instead of putting me down."

Answer: We know this problem first hand and we have learned the hard way that *permanent losing is a matter of commitment to the Lord who wants us in the shape he intended.**

Your husband's reaction is natural for some men. There are others who apparently don't mind. But since your man does mind, let's hope you can get yourself back to those former curves which made you sexually attractive in the original.

For us, keeping the body in shape is a big thing. It calls for commitment, sacrifice, and dedicated attention to whatever is necessary toward that end.

There are doctors and groups who specialize in weight control and you would do well to seek out their assistance.

UNDERGARMENTS

Negative "Here's one thing which puzzles me. Why would my wife be so careless about her undergarments? I mean holes in the girdle, safety pins holding her bra together, a ragged slip. Every time we're together and someone tells her she's

---

* See *The Fat Is in Your Head* by Charlie Shedd (Waco: Word Books, 1972).

attractive, which she is, I can't help thinking how it is underneath. I have a good job and she has plenty of money for clothes."

Positive   "One thing I like about my husband is all the colorful undershorts he buys. I don't mean anything weird, but colors and designs, pictures and prints. Why do I like that? I'll tell you why. It's because this is one more indicator that he has some pride. But also he tells me, 'I think I should look good somewhere just for you.' Isn't that nice?"

"Too Tired"

One of the most common excuses for not responding sexually is, "I'm too tired." We hear it most often from a lonesome husband complaining about his wife's lack of interest. But wives also tell us, "My husband says he's too tired . . . worn out . . . bushed."

Jesus said, "As we think, so we are." Unless we guard against it, we may be taken in by the mistaken mind set which says: "Sex depletes energies."

For us the very reverse is true and it began to be true when we decided to affirm sex as a part of our rest.

Suggestion: In your head when you total your hours of sleep, add an extra hour when you make love. Surprising what this little turn of mind will do for you. "As we think so we are."

Item: We also think sex is good for headaches.

Sex As Reward

Question: "Do you think it is wrong to use sex as a reward for good behavior?" "What do you think of a wife who only yields when she wants something?" These quotes could go on interminably.

Answer: We think bartering of any kind in marriage is loaded with danger. Celebration in the bedroom plays better to the theme, "We love each other freely without price."

"The Joy Of"

Question: "I've been married eleven years and at least I can say this: I've never refused my husband one time. Before we married, one of my aunts had a long talk with me and she told me this was my duty. Believe me, I have always done my duty, and I always intend to."

> She had come for consultation, because her husband was "getting ideas about other women." (Her words.)

Comment: He probably was "getting ideas."

We hear them often, these "I always do my duty" wives, and usually they say it as if they expected a medal. Certainly we do what we do sometimes because we think we should. There are many "should's" in the Christian life. But for a genuine celebration we like Catherine's word. Catherine is a beautiful woman, very turned-on to the Lord, to Jim, to all the good things in her world.

"My mother taught me that wives could be divided into

two kinds, 'the duty of' or 'the joy of.' She said house-keeping was like that, 'duty of' or 'joy of.' So was cooking, entertaining, and especially sex. She said if you ever lost your 'joy of' attitude in sex, you might even lose your husband."

Prayer before Sex?

Question: "My wife thinks we should pray every time before we have intercourse. To me this is weird. Frankly, when I'm ready for sex, to stop and pray throws me off. Your comment?"

Answer: We know some couples who always pray before intercourse, especially one couple. And here's an interesting touch. They report that their prayers always include this phrase: "Help us not to make a baby." They both work and they don't want children yet.

If your wife insists on prayer before intercourse, ask her to pray silently so she can turn on without turning you off.

Generally, stopping to pray before intercourse wouldn't be our thing either. For us prayer is not so much a request before an act as it is a part of our total relationship.

"Then God created male and female, and behold it was excellent in every way."

"Charlie Shedd is a principal war correspondent at the sexual revolution front."

Orlando *Sentinel*

". . . combines openness with a Christian perspective."

Catholic Standard & Times

"Dr. Shedd refrains from moralizing about sex or quoting ancient commandments regarding it. But his approach is deeply Christian in its sympathy, understanding and basic viewpoint."

Baptist Times of Great Britain

"This man has good sense, a wholesome and realistic philosophy, and an easy style of writing."

Houston *Post*

"Charlie Shedd is blunt, direct, and perceptive, but always kind, loving and informative."

Austin *American-Statesman*